My Heart Cries Out to Thee

My Heart Cries Out to Thee

John Charles Duffy

First Printing: July, 2000

International Standard Book Number:
0-88290-690-9

Horizon Publishers' Catalog and Order Number:
1266

Printed and distributed
in the United States of America by

& Distributors, Incorporated

Mailing Address:
P.O. Box 490
Bountiful, Utah 84011-0490

Street Address:
50 South 500 West
Bountiful, Utah 84010

Local Phone: (801) 295-9451
WATS (toll free): 1 (800) 453-0812
FAX: (801) 295-0196

E-mail: horizonp@burgoyne.com
Internet: http:// www.horizonpublishers.biz

Contents

Section 1
The Joy of Worship

Section 2
The Joy of the Spirit

Section 3
The Joy of Service

Introduction

How This Book Came to Be

The prophet Jacob speaks of "the pleasing word of God, yea, the word which healeth the wounded soul" (Jacob 2:8). All of us, no doubt, could identity particular passages of scripture which have afforded us healing in times of heartache, comfort in times of grief, or encouragement in times of adversity. All of us, no doubt, have at one time or another had the experience of stumbling upon a passage of scripture that expressed perfectly our own feelings of gratitude or adoration. All of us, no doubt, have favorite passages of scripture which motivate us to service and well doing.

I have a childhood memory of sitting in Sacrament Meeting reading a tiny volume of selected Bible verses—probably a gift from my Protestant grandmother on the occasion of my baptism. I recall encountering in the back of the volume a list of biblical references appropriate to certain moments in one's life: at a parting of loved ones, at a birth, at a death, for times of sorrow, for times of joy, for times of pain, when feeling angry, when feeling alone, when feeling overwhelmed, and so on.

As a Latter-day Saint, I have found myself at times wishing I had such a list for the scriptures of the Restoration: the Book of Mormon, Doctrine and Covenants, and the Pearl of Great Price. We have, of course, the Topical Guide, which serves as a selective concordance and a compendium of scriptural passages organized by gospel theme: Adversity, Eternal Marriage, Melchizedek Priesthood, Premortal Life, and so on. I have thought it would be useful to have also a compendium of scriptural passages organized by different kinds of needs: the need to be comforted after a loss, the need to be reassured in times of uncertainty, the need to feel competent, the need to feel loved, the need to know that our remorse has brought forgiveness, the need to give thanks for blessings received, the need to be reminded of our call to serve.

How This Book Could Be Used

Shortly after I began compiling the passages which appear in this book, I received a call from a friend, informing me that her father had finally passed away after a prolonged period of illness. I never know what to say in that situation, but we talked for a while. I asked how she was coping. She said that they were receiving wonderful support from ward members. She confessed she felt somewhat relieved that the stress of her father's illness had finally ended. She was handling things, she assured me.

I knew enough about the grief process to realize that her feeling of "handling things" wasn't going to last. Eventually, ward members were going to go on with their lives and expect my friend and her family to do the same. A feeling of isolation was likely to set in, and it was then that my friend would probably begin to feel the enormity of the loss of her father. She might come to feel guilty for her initial feelings of relief. As the oldest (and most successful) child in her family, she would likely find herself shouldering burdens for other family members. She would be asked to expend energy on their behalf, at precisely the time when she would need to reserve energy for her own mourning.

I sat down at my computer that night, called up the scriptures I'd begun to compile, and copied forty or fifty of the passages onto small notes. I sealed each note up separately and gave each its own label: "When you're feeling alone," "When you're feeling down," "When you're feeling worn out." I mailed her the notes in a packet the next day, with a letter explaining that while she might not feel the need for these now, she might find them useful in the near future.

That is the kind of need this book was created to serve.

Who the Book Is Written For

My Heart Cries Out to Thee has been compiled with two different audiences in mind.

First, the book is intended as a resource for Latter-day Saints themselves—a collection of brief, moving, memorable thoughts of the kind that might be easily memorized to be recalled throughout the day, taped to a mirror, penned inside a condolences card, passed on as a note to a friend who's feeling down, printed in a ward bulletin, reflected upon during the sacrament, discussed during a bishop's interview, used to set the tone for family prayer, adopted as the slogan of a youth retreat, recited at the close of a missionary zone conference, set to music, copied out in calligraphy, or rendered in needlepoint, to be framed on a wall. Particular emphasis is laid on passages of the scriptures which speak to people in times of discouragement, loneliness, heartache, anxiety, uncertainty—passages which fit Jacob's description of "the pleasing word of God, yea, the word which healeth the wounded soul" (Jacob 2:8).

Second, the book is intended as a means of sharing the joy of the Restoration with individuals outside our faith community who may not be interested, at this stage of their lives, in formally investigating the Church. There is much in the scriptures of the Restoration to which members of other faith traditions could relate at once—messages and sentiments akin to (if not identical to) those they know from the texts they already regard as sacred. I have included in *My Heart Cries Out to Thee* passages that I could see myself sharing with my own non-member family members, friends, and co-workers in an atmosphere of mutual appreciation of each other's faith traditions. It is my hope that the book may thus serve as a resource for building bridges with those with whom, in the words of M. Russell Ballard, "we [have] pleasantly agree[d] to disagree . . . on certain points of doctrine, while [uniting] with them in the great common denominators of faith in God and benevolent service to others" (*Ensign*, June 1998, p. 63).

How the Book is Organized

My Heart Cries Out to Thee is organized into three main sections, to reflect the stages of the process by which disciples of the Lord achieve that "exceedingly great joy" exemplified by the people of King Benjamin (Mosiah 5:4). As recounted in the opening chapters of the Book of Mosiah, the first stage of that process is worship—to "render all the thanks and praise which your whole soul has power to possess to that God who has created you" (Mosiah 2:20) and to come before the Lord in a spirit of humility and supplication (see Mosiah 4:1-2). The first section of this book, "The Joy of Worship," contains expressions of praise, supplication, and thanksgiving related to this dimension of our discipleship.

In the second stage of the process, the Spirit comes upon King Benjamin's people, causing them to be "filled with joy, having received a remission of their sins, and having peace of conscience" (Mosiah 4:3). King Benjamin reports that as a result of this spiritual experience, the people "come to a knowledge of the goodness of God, and his matchless power, and his wisdom, and his patience, and his long suffering towards [them]" (Mosiah 4:6).

The second section of this book, "The Joy of the Spirit," contains scriptural assurances that we, too, can experience the comfort, power, direction, and peace which come from our Father in Heaven, through the grace of the Savior.

In the third stage of the process, the people take upon themselves a covenant to serve God "all the remainder of [their] days" (Mosiah 5:5). King Benjamin teaches them that this commitment is synonymous with spending their lives "in the service of [their] fellow beings" (Mosiah 2:17). More specifically, King Benjamin charges the people to "live peaceably, [rendering] to every man according to his due" (Mosiah 4:13), and to "impart of [their] substance to the poor, every man according to that which he hath, such as feeding the hungry, clothing the naked, visiting the sick and administering to their relief" (Mosiah 4:26). The third section of this book, "The Joy of Service," contains exhortations and promises related to this final dimension of our discipleship.

Notes on the Text

The prayers and inspirational thoughts in this book are drawn from the scriptures, but they rarely represent complete, word-for-word quotations, as will quickly become evident to anyone who looks up the chapter-and-verse citations which appear in the footnotes. There are several reasons for this:

1. In compiling thoughts that related to a particular topic, or that spoke to a particular need, I excerpted only those portions of a verse which applied to the topic or need at hand. A passage in this book may therefore be composed of phrases from multiple verses of scriptures which were thematically linked in the original, though separated by intervening material. For the purposes of this book, the intervening material has not been quoted.

2. Some words or phrases from a passage may not have been included in the excerpt simply for brevity's sake. Such words and phrases include "and," "behold," and "it came to pass."

3. Because the excerpted passages lack their original context, it has often been necessary to insert, or replace, words or phrases for the sake of clarification. For instance, a pronoun ("he") might be replaced with its antecedent ("the Lord"), as specified in a previous, unquoted verse.

4. In a few cases, a word from the original has been replaced with another in order to highlight one of several meanings conveyed by that word, or to avoid an infelicitous interpretation. In an excerpt from D&C 35:13, for instance, the phrase "thrash the nations" has been rendered as "reprove the nations" so as not to give the wrong impression.

5. On occasion, I have taken the liberty of transposing whole phrases. In some cases, this is for the sake of clarity: an ambiguous pronoun such as "this" might be replaced with a phrase some lines away to clarify what "this" refers to.

6. In other cases, the transposition serves to emphasize those elements of the passage which speak to a particular theme. For instance, in an excerpt from 1 Ne. 11:17 ("I know that [God] loveth his children; nevertheless, I do not know the meaning of all things"), I have reversed the order of the two clauses ("I do not know the meaning of all things; nevertheless, I know that [God] loveth his children"), to direct the reader's attention more closely to the passage's affirmation of God's love.

7. In a very few instances, a transposition may occur for stylistic effect. For example: under the heading "Promises of Peace," I wanted to include a clause from 3 Nephi 22:13 (". . . and great shall be the peace of thy children"),

plus the first clause of the next verse ("In righteousness shalt thou be established"). In their excerpted form, these clauses sounded clumsy until I placed them in reverse order.

8. In the interest of likening the scriptures to ourselves, I have frequently adapted the language of the original to make a passage speak more directly to readers, or to highlight a passage's applicability to a variety of situations (a technique familiar to anyone who has studied the *Missionary Guide*). "He" might become "you," for instance; "they" might become "we."

9. Similarly, I have rendered some passages in the imperative rather than the indicative mood, so that a description of a praiseworthy action becomes an exhortation to action (or vice-versa). In other cases, pronouns and verb tenses may be adapted so that, for instance, a promise that something will happen becomes a prayer for the fulfillment of that promise.

10. Following the lead of James E. Faust, Neal A. Maxwell, Jeffrey R. Holland, Elaine L. Jack, Chieko N. Okazaki and others, I have incorporated gender-inclusive language into all my excerpts from the scriptures. I have tried, however, to do so without destroying the cadence of the original language. Rather than replace a line such as "*men* should be anxiously engaged" with the unwieldy alternative "*men and women* should be anxiously engaged," I have instead inserted a gender-neutral pronoun: "*you* should be anxiously engaged."

11. In other cases, I have made an excerpt gender-inclusive by replacing one scriptural phrase with a different scriptural phrase. "Children of men," for example, might become "inhabitants of the earth"; "trust no man" might become "trust not in the arm of flesh."

12. Since punctuation is not a fixed element of the text (i.e., punctuation in the scriptures differs from one

edition to another), I have been free in adapting the punctuation of the excerpts as need or style dictated.

None of these textual changes alters the essential meaning of the original. Indeed, these are techniques which any author might use in citing a passage of scripture. Normally an author would indicate such changes through the use of ellipses (. . .) and square brackets, or by setting quotation marks around phrases from the original which have been incorporated, not in their original order, into a sentence of the author's own making.

I have opted not to use these conventional devices, however, in order to avoid giving the excerpts a "cluttered" look. Instead, I have arranged the excerpts as if they were lines of free verse. This has the double virtue of (1) highlighting the poetic quality of many of these passages, and (2) serving as a red flag to readers that these excerpts do not claim to be precise reproductions of the original text (which, of course, takes the form of prose). I thus advise the readers that each passage is to be *compared* to the verse or verses cited, if they feel a concern for word-for-word accuracy.

Section 1

The Joy of Worship

"Worship [Christ]," Nephi exhorts us, "with all your might, mind, and strength, and your whole soul" (2 Ne. 25:29). For Latter-day Saints, worship occurs in various settings. We worship as individuals, pouring out our souls to God in the solitude of our own closets. We worship as families, by observing such traditions as family prayer and scripture study. Even Family Home Evening can be an act of worship if it directs the thoughts of family members to our Savior and our Father in Heaven. We worship as local faith communities when we meet weekly to partake of the sacrament. We worship as a global church when heads worldwide bow in prayer at the opening and closing of each session of General Conference, viewed via satellite or on videotape. Our most sacred worship, of course, occurs in the temple, when we recommit ourselves to the sacred obligations of our discipleship, and unite in prayer around the temple altar on behalf of loved ones and strangers in need.

Worship is an act of praise, meaning heartfelt acknowledgement of the greatness and goodness of God. The authors of the scriptures both invite us to join them in praise and provide examples of how to do so, including that ancient expression of praise called the "hosanna" (Hebrew for "Save, we pray"). James E. Talmage explained that lifting our hearts in praise to God helps us to "develop that abiding faith, such as shall lead to repentance."[1] For this reason, perhaps, Neal A. Maxwell has recommended that we "have as the purpose of some prayers sheer adoration."[2] We praise God for his greatness, taking comfort in the assurance that because he is

1. *Sunday Night Talks by Radio*, 2nd ed., Salt Lake City: The Church of Jesus Christ of Latter-day Saints, 1931, p. 438.
2. In Spencer W. Kimball *et al.*, *Prayer*, Salt Lake City: Deseret Book Co., 1977, p. 47; quoted in *Ensign*, Oct. 95, p. 16.

infinitely great, our trust in him cannot fail. We praise him for his love, and in doing so are naturally led to ponder how well that love is reflected in our own relationships with others. As a corollary to our knowledge that God's love for his children knows no boundaries, we rejoice in the recognition that all who seek with honest heart, whatever their faith tradition, "receive a portion of God's light" to "help them on their way to eternal salvation."[3]

Acknowledging God's greatness and love, we are naturally inclined to approach him in prayer and supplication, laying the desires of our hearts before him for judgment, confident that he will grant us whatever lies in our best interests. Knowing that Christ himself prays to the Father on our behalf when we stumble along the way, we find the courage to pick ourselves up and overcome our mistakes, asking God's forgiveness and mercy. We pray for grace to "compensate for our deficiencies,"[4] for strength to confront difficult circumstances, for assistance in carrying out God's work, for comfort in times of grief or anxiety. Recognizing that we "lack the capacity to develop a Christlike nature by our own effort alone,"[5] we can pray for spiritual qualities such as faith and charity. We can pray for healing, whether our ailment be physical or spiritual, and for blessings, both temporal and spiritual, to rest upon our homes.

Worship implies thanksgiving for those blessings which we have received, even those blessings which, in the words of Howard W. Hunter, "do not look or feel like blessings."[6] As Neal A. Maxwell has recommended that we dedicate some of our prayers entirely to praise, so

---

3. Statement of the First Presidency regarding God's Love for All Mankind, 15 Feb. 1978; quoted in *Ensign*, Jan. 1988, p. 48.
4. Chieko N. Okazaki, *Ensign*, Nov. 1993, p. 96.
5. Bruce C. Hafen, *Ensign*, Dec. 1993, p. 12.
6. *Ensign*, Nov. 1987, p. 58.

Ezra Taft Benson suggested that we "devote more of our prayers to expressions of gratitude and thanksgiving for blessings already received."[7] We can give thanks for the Atonement, and for the blessings it brings into our day-to-day lives; for answered prayers, though the answer may not have been the one we had hoped for; for the success we have enjoyed in carrying out the Lord's work, though that, too, may not have been all we had hoped for; for protection in our daily walk, in ways we do not always recognize.

Finally, an important element of worship has long been the invoking of a benediction upon those assembled. Worshippers thus carry back with them into the world words of blessing to be recalled later as a source of comfort and strength. Such benedictions have traditionally been used to close not only worship services, but also letters (the epistles of Paul, for instance) and partings between friends or family members.

---

7. *God, Family, Country,* Salt Lake City: Deseret Book Co., 1974, p. 199; see also *Ensign,* May 1994, p. 27.

Praise

Invitations to Praise

Blessed be the name of our God;
    let us sing to his praise.
Let us give thanks to his holy name,
    for he doth work righteousness forever.[1]

We will glory in the Lord;
    we will rejoice, for our joy is full.
Yea, we will praise our God forever.
    Who can glory too much in the Lord?[2]

Sing praises unto the Lord all the day long,
    and when the night comes,
cease not to praise him,
    because of the multitude of his tender mercies.[3]

Pray unto the Lord, call upon his holy name,
    make known his wonderful works
among the people.[4]

1. Alma 26:8
2. Alma 26:16

3. Ether 6:9, 12
4. D&C 65:4

*G*lory and honor and power and might
    be ascribed to our God;
for he is full of mercy, justice, grace, truth,
    and peace forever and ever.[1]

*L*et the earth break forth into singing!
    Let the dead speak forth anthems of eternal praise!
Let the mountains shout for joy,
    and all ye valleys cry aloud,
and all ye seas and dry lands
    tell the wonders of your Eternal King!
Ye rivers, brooks, and rills, flow down with gladness!
    Let the woods and all the trees of the field
    praise the Lord,
and ye solid rocks weep for joy!
    Let the sun, moon, and the morning stars
    sing together,
and all the children of God shout for joy!
    And let the eternal creations
declare his name forever and ever![2]

---

1. D&C 84:102   2. D&C 128:22-23

Expressions of Praise

Great and marvelous are thy works,
    O Lord God Almighty!
Thy throne is high in the heavens,
    and thy power, and goodness, and mercy
are over all the inhabitants of the earth.[1]

❧

O Lord, I will praise thee forever;
    yea, my soul will rejoice in thee,
my God, and the rock of my salvation.[2]

❧

O Lord, I will praise thee;
    thou comfortest me.[3]

❧

My soul delighteth to prophesy;
    my heart doth magnify God's holy name.[4]

❧

O Lord, thou hast all power,
    and can do whatsoever thou wilt
for our benefit.[5]

❧

---

1. 1 Ne. 1:14   3. 2 Ne. 22:1   5. Ether 3:4
2. 2 Ne. 4:30   4. 2 Ne. 25:13

O Lord God Almighty, thou sittest enthroned
    with glory, honor, power, majesty,
might, dominion, truth, justice,
    judgment, mercy and an infinity of fulness,
from everlasting to everlasting.[1]

*W*e shall mention the loving kindness of our Lord,
    and all that he has bestowed upon us
according to his goodness,
    forever and ever.[2]

Hosannas

*H*osanna to the Lord, the most high God,
    for he is God over all the earth.[3]

*H*osanna! Blessed be the name of the Most High God![4]

*H*osanna, hosanna,
    blessed be the name of the Lord God![5]

*H*elp us by the power of thy Spirit,
    that we may mingle our voices
with those bright, shining seraphs around thy throne,
    with acclamations of praise, singing:
Hosanna to God and the Lamb! Amen and Amen.[6]

1. D&C 109:77   3. 1 Ne. 11:6   5. D&C 19:37
2. D&C 133:52   4. 3 Ne. 11:17   6. D&C 109:79-80

Declarations of God's Greatness

How great the goodness of our God,
the plan of our God,
the justice of our God,
the mercy of our God,
the holiness of our God—
the Lord God is his name.[1]

My joy is carried away,
even unto boasting in my God,
for he has all power, all wisdom,
and all understanding;
he comprehendeth all things and is a merciful Being.
Blessed is the name of my God![2]

Are not the things that God hath wrought
marvelous in our eyes?
Who can comprehend the marvelous works of God?[3]

Hear, O ye heavens, and give ear, O earth:
The Lord is God,
and beside him there is no Savior.
Great is his wisdom, marvelous are his ways,
and the extent of his doings none can find out.
His purposes fail not,
neither are there any who can stay his hand.
From eternity to eternity he is the same,
and his years never fail.[4]

---

1. 2 Ne. 9:10, 13, 17, 19-20, 41   3. Morm. 9:16
2. Alma 26:35-36   4. D&C 76:1-4

The earth rolls upon her wings,
    the sun giveth his light by day,
the moon giveth her light by night,
    and the stars also give their light,
as they roll upon their wings
    in the midst of the power of God.
Behold, all these are kingdoms,
    and any who hath seen the least of these
hath seen God moving in majesty and power.[1]

Declarations of God's Love for All People

All the earth shall see the salvation of the Lord;
    every nation, kindred, tongue and people
    shall be blessed.[2]

The whole earth is full of the glory of the Lord.[3]

God is mindful of every people,
    whatsoever land they may be in;
yea, he numbereth his people,
    and his bowels of mercy are over all the earth.[4]

---

1. D&C 88:45, 47
2. 1 Ne. 19:17

3. 2 Ne. 16:3
4. Alma 26:37

The voice of the Lord is unto the ends of the earth,
    that all who will hear may hear.[1]

❧

Let a feast of fat things be prepared for the poor;
    a feast of fat things, of wine well refined;
a supper of the house of the Lord, well prepared,
    unto which all nations shall be invited:
the rich and the learned, the wise and the noble,
    the poor, the lame, the blind, and the deaf—
all these shall come in unto the marriage of the Lamb,
    and partake of the supper of the Lord.[2]

❧

All things which come of the earth
    are made for the benefit and use
of the whole human family,
    both to please the eye and to gladden the heart;
for food and for raiment, for taste and for smell,
    to strengthen the body and to enliven the soul.
And it pleaseth God that he hath given
    all these things unto us;
for unto this end were they made to be used,
    with judgment, not to excess,
neither by extortion.[3]

❧

The Lord is my God, and your God,
    and we are all his children.[4]

❧

We believe in doing good to all.[5]

❧

---

1. D&C 1:11   3. D&C 59:18-20   5. A of F 1:13
2. D&C 58:8-11   4. Moses 6:43

Recognitions of the Good Outside Our Own Faith Community

I command all people,
     both in the east and in the west,
in the north and in the south,
     and in the islands of the sea,
that they shall write the words
     which I speak unto them;
for I speak unto all according to their language,
     unto their understanding.[1]

*W*hatsoever thing persuadeth to do good is of me;
     for good cometh of none save it be of me.
For behold, I am the light, and the life,
     and the truth of the world.[2]

*E*very thing which inviteth and enticeth to do good,
     and to love God, and to serve him,
     is inspired of God.
Wherefore, take heed that ye do not judge
     that which is good and of God to be of the devil.[3]

*B*ehold, there are diverse ways
     that God doth manifest himself
unto the inhabitants of the earth, which are good;
     and all things which are good cometh of Christ.[4]

---

1. 2 Ne. 29:11; 31:3
2. Ether 4:12

3. Moro. 7:13-14
4. Moro. 7:24

*D*eny not the gifts of God, for they are many,
   and they come from the same God.
There are different ways
   that these gifts are administered,
but it is the same God who worketh all in all;
   and they are given by the manifestations
of the Spirit of God, to profit us.[1]

❧

*R*emember that every good gift cometh of Christ.[2]

❧

*N*ow, behold, I will bring this part of my gospel
   to the knowledge of this people.
I do not bring it to destroy that which they
   have received, but to build it up.[3]

❧

*T*he Spirit giveth light to everyone that cometh
   into the world; and the Spirit enlighteneth
everyone that cometh into the world;
   and everyone that hearkeneth
to the voice of the Spirit cometh unto God.[4]

❧

*W*e allow all persons the privilege to worship
   according to the dictates of their own conscience,
let them worship how, where, or what they may.[5]

❧

*I*f there is anything of good report or praiseworthy,
   we seek after these things.[6]

❧

---

1. Moro. 10:8   3. D&C 10:52   5. A of F 1:11
2. Moro. 10:18   4. D&C 84:46-47   6. A of F 1:13

Prayer and Supplication

Christ's Intercessory Prayer Before the Father

Father,
    behold the sufferings and death
of him who did not sin,
    in whom thou wast well pleased.

Behold the blood of thy Son which was shed,
    the blood of him whom thou gavest
that thyself might be glorified.

Wherefore, Father,
    spare these my brothers and sisters
that believe on my name,
    that they may come unto me
and have everlasting life.[1]

---

1. D&C 45:4-5

Prayers for Forgiveness and Mercy

Have mercy on me,
according to the multitude of thy tender mercies.[1]

❧

O have mercy, and apply the atoning blood of Christ
that we may receive forgiveness of our sins,
and our hearts may be purified.[2]

❧

O Jesus, thou Son of God,
have mercy on me,
who am in the gall of bitterness.[3]

❧

O Lord, forgive my unworthiness,
and remember my brothers and sisters in mercy.[4]

❧

O Jehovah,
have mercy upon this people,
and as all sin,
forgive our transgressions,
and let them be blotted out forever.[5]

❧

O Lord God Almighty,
maker of heaven, earth, and seas,
and of all things that in them are—
stretch forth thy hand,
let thine ear be inclined,
let thy heart be softened,
and thy bowels moved with compassion toward me.[6]

❧

---

1. 1 Ne. 8:8   3. Alma 36:18   5. D&C 109:34
2. Mosiah 4:2   4, Alma 38:14   6. D&C 121:4

*B*e merciful unto thy servant, O God.[1]

❧

O Lord, wilt thou not have compassion?[2]

❧

J ask thee, O Lord,
 in the name of thine Only Begotten,
even Jesus Christ,
 that thou wilt have mercy.[3]

❧

Prayers for Grace

O Lord, wilt thou redeem my soul?
 Wilt thou make me that I may shake
 at the appearance of sin?
May the gates of hell be shut continually before me,
 because my heart is broken and my spirit
 is contrite!
Wilt thou encircle me around in the robe
 of thy righteousness!
Wilt thou clear my way before me!
 O Lord, I have trusted in thee,
 and I will trust in thee forever.
I will not put my trust in the arm of flesh;
 I will cry unto thee, my God,
 the rock of my righteousness.[4]

❧

---

1. Moses 1:36
2. Moses 7:49
3. Moses 7:50
4. 2 Ne. 4:31-35

*M*ay God grant, in his great fulness,
    that we might be brought unto repentance
    and good works,
that we might be restored unto grace for grace.[1]

❧

*C*ondemn me not because of mine imperfection.[2]

❧

O Lord, do not be angry with thy servant
    because of my weakness before thee.[3]

❧

*H*oly Father,
    we ask thee to assist us, thy people,
    with thy grace,
that we may be found worthy in thy sight
    to secure a fulfilment of the promises
which thou hast made unto us.[4]

❧

O Lord, remember thy servant,
    that I have sincerely striven to do thy will.[5]

❧

---

1. Hel. 12:24   3. Ether 3:2   5. D&C 109:68
2. Morm. 9:31   4. D&C 109:10-11

Prayers for Strength

O Lord, according to my faith which is in thee,
    wilt thou give me strength.[1]

*H*ow long shall we suffer these great afflictions,
    O Lord?
O Lord, give us strength
    according to our faith, which is in Christ.[2]

O Lord, wilt thou give me strength,
    that I may bear with mine infirmities.[3]

*S*trengthen us and prepare us,
    lest we enter into temptation.[4]

*S*trengthen up thy people,
    whithersoever they are found.[5]

*S*trengthen us by thy word,
    and let no one hinder us
doing that which thou hast appointed unto us.[6]

---

1. 1 Ne. 7:17
2. Alma 14:26
3. Alma 31:30
4. D&C 31:8, 12
5. D&C 37:2
6. D&C 50:37-38

Prayers for Assistance In Carrying Out God's Work

O Lord, pour out thy Spirit upon thy servant,
    that I may do this work with holiness of heart.[1]

❧

O Lord, have mercy,
    that I may be an instrument in thy hands.[2]

❧

O Lord, wilt thou comfort my soul,
    and give unto me success,
and also my fellow laborers who are with me—
    all these wilt thou comfort, O Lord.
Yea, wilt thou comfort their souls in Christ.[3]

❧

May the kingdom of God go forth,
    that the kingdom of heaven may come,
that thou, O God, mayest be glorified
    in heaven so on earth;
for thine is the honor, power, and glory,
    forever and ever.[4]

❧

---

1. Mosiah 18:12   3. Alma 31:32
2. Alma 2:30   4. D&C 65:6

Especially for the Parents of Missionaries

J rejoice exceedingly, that your Lord Jesus Christ
    hath been mindful of you,
and hath called you to his holy work.
    I am mindful of you always in my prayers,
continually praying unto God the Father
    in the name of his Holy Child, Jesus,
that he, through his infinite goodness and grace,
    will keep you through the endurance of faith
    on his name to the end.[1]

Prayers for Comfort

J am encompassed about; my heart groaneth.
    O Lord, wilt thou encircle me
    in the robe of thy righteousness![2]

O Lord, my heart is exceedingly sorrowful;
    wilt thou comfort my soul in Christ.[3]

*H*elp me to say,
    with thy grace assisting me:
Thy will be done, O Lord,
    and not mine.[4]

O God, where art thou?
    Let thy hiding place no longer be covered.[5]

---

1. Moro. 8:2-3   3. Alma 31:31   5. D&C 121:1, 4
2. 2 Ne. 4:18-19, 33   4. D&C 109:44

A Prayer for Faith

O God,
    if there is a God,
and if thou art God,
    wilt thou make thyself known unto me,
and I will give away all my sins to know thee.[1]

A Prayer for Love

I pray unto the Father with all the energy of heart,
    that I may be filled with this love,
which he doth bestow upon all
    who are true followers of his Son, Jesus Christ;
that when he shall appear I shall be like him,
    for I shall see him as he is;
that I may have this hope,
    that I may be purified even as he is pure. Amen.[2]

A Prayer for Healing

O Lord my God, have mercy on me,
    and heal me according to my faith,
    which is in Christ.[3]

---

1. Alma 22:18   2. Moro. 7:48   3. Alma 15:10

A Prayer for Dedicating a Home

Do thou grant, Holy Father,
    that this house may be a house of prayer,
a house of fasting, a house of faith,
    a house of glory and of God.[1]

---

1. D&C 109:14, 16

Thanksgiving and Blessing

Thanksgiving for the Atonement

Behold, the Lord hath redeemed my soul;
   I am encircled about eternally in the arms
   of his love.[1]

I have repented of my sins,
   and have been redeemed of the Lord;
behold, I am born of the Spirit.[2]

O blessed Jesus, who has saved me
   from an awful hell!
O blessed God, have mercy on this people![3]

I thank my great God that he has given me
   a portion of his spirit to soften my heart,
and that he hath granted unto me that I might repent,
   and that he hath forgiven me my sins
and taken away the guilt from my heart,
   through the merits of his Son.[4]

---

1. 2 Ne. 1:15
2. Mosiah 27:24

3. Alma 19:29
4. Alma 24:8, 10

𝐽n thee is my joy,
for thou hast turned thy judgments
away from me,
because of thy Son.[1]

※

𝒯he Righteous is lifted up,
and the Lamb is slain from the foundation
of the world,
and I am in the bosom of the Father.[2]

※

𝒯hanksgiving for Answered Prayers

𝐽 remember what the Lord has done for me,
yea, that he hath heard my prayer;
I remember his merciful arm
which he extended towards me.[3]

※

𝒯hou art merciful unto thy children
when they cry unto thee,
and thou dost hear them.[4]

※

𝒜s we have assembled ourselves together
and have asked the Father in Christ's name,
even so we have received.[5]

※

𝒯he alms of our prayers
have come up into the ears of the Lord.[6]

※

---

1. Alma 33:11   3. Alma 29:10   5. D&C 42:3
2. Moses 7:47   4. Alma 33:8   6. D&C 88:2

Thy servant has sought thee earnestly;
now I have found thee.[1]

Thanksgiving for Success in God's Work

After much tribulation,
the Lord did hear my cries,
and did answer my prayers,
and has made me an instrument in his hands.[2]

Behold, how great reason we have to rejoice;
for could we have supposed when we started
that God would have granted unto us
such great blessings?
And this is the blessing
which hath been bestowed upon us,
that we have been made instruments
in the hands of God
to bring about this work.[3]

I do not boast in my own strength,
nor in my own wisdom;
but my joy is full,
yea, my heart is brim with joy,
and I will rejoice in my God,
for in his strength I can do all things.
This is my joy and my great thanksgiving,
and I will give thanks unto my God forever.[4]

---

1. Abr. 2:12
2. Mosiah 23:10
3. Alma 26:1, 3
4. Alma 26:11-12, 37

God hath given me a holy calling,
  and hath given me much success,
in the which my joy is full.
  But I do not joy in my own success alone;
my joy is more full
  because of the success of my fellow laborers.[1]

Thanks be to thy name,
  O Lord God of Israel,
who keepest covenant
  and showest mercy unto thy servants.[2]

Thanksgiving for Divine Protection

I know of a surety that the Lord
  hath protected us and delivered us:
thanks be unto God.[3]

We ought to thank our God,
  who has kept and preserved us,
and has granted that we should live in peace.[4]

Blessed be the name of our God,
  who has been mindful of us,
wanderers in a strange land.[5]

---

1. Alma 29:13-14   3. 1 Ne. 5:8-9   5. Alma 26:36
2. D&C 109:1   4. Mosiah 2:19-20

*W*hen I lie down at night,
   I lie down unto the Lord,
that he may watch over me in my sleep;
   and when I rise in the morning,
my heart is full of thanks unto God.[1]

*E*ternity was our covering
   and our rock, as we journeyed.[2]

---

1. Alma 37:37   2. Abr. 2:16

Benedictions

May the Spirit of the Lord be poured upon you,
  and may he grant unto you eternal life
through the redemption of Christ,
  whom he has prepared
from the foundation of the world.[1]

May the Lord bless you,
  and keep your garments spotless,
that ye may at last be brought to sit down
  with Abraham, Isaac, and Jacob,
and the holy prophets
  who have been ever since the world began,
having your garments spotless
  even as their garments are spotless,
in the kingdom of heaven, to go no more out.[2]

May the peace of God rest upon you,
  and all that you possess,
according to your faith and good works,
  from this time forth and forever.[3]

May God grant unto you
  that your burdens may be light,
through the joy of his Son.[4]

---

1. Mosiah 18:13   3. Alma 7:27
2. Alma 7:25   4. Alma 33:23

May the Lord bless your soul,
    and receive you at the last day into his kingdom,
to sit down in peace.[1]

※

May the grace of God the Father,
    and also the Lord Jesus Christ,
and the Holy Ghost, which beareth record of them,
    be and abide in you forever.[2]

※

May Christ lift thee up,
    and may his sufferings and death,
and his mercy and long-suffering,
    and the hope of his glory and of eternal life,
rest in your mind forever.[3]

※

May the grace of God the Father,
    whose throne is high in the heavens,
and our Lord Jesus Christ,
    who sitteth on the right hand of his power,
be and abide with you forever.[4]

Especially for a Time of Death

May God raise you from death
    by the power of the resurrection,
and from everlasting death
    by the power of the atonement,
that ye may be received into the eternal
    kingdom of God,
that ye may praise him through grace divine.[5]

※

---

1. Alma 38:15   3. Moro. 9:25   5. 2 Ne. 10:25
2. Ether 12:41   4. Moro. 9:26

Especially for Missionaries

May God grant unto you
that you may sit down in the kingdom of God,
and also all those who are the fruit of your labors,
that you may go no more out,
but that you may praise him forever.[1]

Especially for National Observances

May the Lord preserve his people in righteousness
and in holiness of heart.
May the God of Abraham, and the God of Isaac,
and the God of Jacob,
protect this people.[2]

1. Alma 29:17   2. 3 Ne. 4:29-30

Section 2

The Joy of the Spirit

The joy of worship is the joy of speaking to God. The joy of the Spirit is the joy of hearing God answer. The Spirit's voice comes to us in a variety of ways: through the scriptures, through prophetic and inspired teachings, through flashes of insight in the course of prayer or study, or simply through the quiet sense of well being that tells us we are walking in the right path.

During his mortal ministry, Jesus spoke of the Spirit as the Comforter (John 14:26); in latter-day revelation, he adds the title, Holy Spirit of promise (D&C 88:3). Both titles remind us that one of the Spirit's chief functions is to provide us with assurance and consolation in times of need.

To those who question their self-worth, God offers assurance of his unconditional love. To the penitent, he affirms his "forgiving, long-suffering, merciful nature"[1]; to perfectionists, his ready acceptance of our honest, though imperfect, efforts. To those who feel inadequate, he promises grace, support, and protection. To those who feel uncertain of their course, he promises guidance and inspiration. To those who feel overwhelmed, he holds out promises of heavenly power and success in his work.

The fulfillment of such promises, however, does not necessarily follow as quickly as we might wish, or in the way that we might have anticipated. As James E. Faust has observed: "It is always gratifying to hear of prayers being answered and miracles occurring in the lives of those who need them. But what of those faithful souls who receive no miracles, whose prayers are not answered in the way they ask?"[2] In such circumstances, it is easy to become depressed or discouraged, bogged down in feelings of failure or self-recrimination. At these moments,

---

1. Jeffrey R. Holland, *Ensign*, April 1998, p. 19.
2. *Ensign*, April 1996, p. 6.

too, the Spirit offers comfort. In the scriptures, we find recorded the words of God himself, urging us take heart, to be patient, to remember our great worth in his eyes; and the scriptural authors add their own testimonies that however unworthy or alone we may imagine ourselves, our Heavenly Father never fails to hear our prayers and is always close at hand. "We need but go to him."[3]

This is not to imagine that the Spirit will somehow make us immune to the heartache, loss, grief, and fears which are part and parcel of mortality. There is no question that "we will have difficulties the way every generation and people have had difficulties,"[4] and that these will cause us pain or deep concern. The Spirit assures us, however, that "there is no burden we need bear alone."[5]

We can draw strength from the knowledge that Christ took upon himself in Gethsemane not only our sins, but also our pains and our sorrows. In some way we cannot entirely understand, Christ suffers with us. His sufferings are our sufferings—not only in the sense that he suffered the penalty of our sins so that we would not have to (see D&C 19:16), but also in the sense that he "knows" our griefs and sicknesses "firsthand."[6]

Perhaps our greatest challenge in the face of loss, anxiety, or perplexity, is to learn to trust that in spite of appearances, God's providence is slowly but surely leading us where we're meant to go. The guidance of the Spirit will not always be dramatic or obvious; the way to achieve our goals and desires will not always be clear. In the words of Howard W. Hunter, "At various times in our lives, probably at repeated times in our lives, we do have to acknowledge that God knows what we do not know and sees what we do not see."[7] During such periods, it is

3. Barbara W. Winder, *Ensign*, June 1988, p. 71.
4. Howard W. Hunter, *Ensign*, Oct. 1993, p. 72.
5. Chieko N. Okazaki, *Ensign*, Nov. 1993, p. 94.
6. Neal A. Maxwell, *Ensign*, May 1997, p. 12.
7. *Ensign*, Nov. 1987, p. 60.

important to maintain a healthy perspective: to accept a certain element of uncertainty in our lives, to avoid over-burdening ourselves, to take the time necessary for rest and reflection, to endure in the course we sense to be right, even at the risk of rejection by others, to trust that inspiration will come in the moment it is needed.

Addressing the saints, Gordon B. Hinckley has said, "I know that many of you carry very heavy burdens. I know that many of you live under extreme stress. I know that you are anxious to do the right thing and that you are prayerfully trying to do so."[8] It is to such individuals that the assurances, condolences, testimonies, and reflections which appear on the following pages are directed.

---

8. *Ensign*, May 1990, p. 68.

Assurances and Promises

Assurances of God's Unconditional Love

Come, every one that thirsteth,
    come ye to the waters;
and you who have no money,
    come buy and eat.
Yea, come buy wine and milk
    without money and without price.[1]

Doth he cry unto any, saying: Depart from me?
    Nay, but he saith,
Come unto me all ye ends of the earth.
    Hath he commanded any
that they should not partake of his salvation?
    Nay, but he hath given it free for all.
Hath the Lord commanded any
    that they should not partake of his goodness?
Nay, but all are privileged the one like unto the other.
    And he denieth none that come unto him,
black and white, bond and free, male and female;
    all are alike unto God.[2]

---

1. 2 Ne. 9:50   2. 2 Ne. 26:25, 27-28, 33

*B*ehold, mine arm of mercy is extended towards you,
   and whosoever will come, will I receive.[1]

*Y*our Father who is in heaven
   maketh his sun to rise
on the evil and on the good.[2]

*E*very one that asketh, receiveth;
   whomsoever seeketh, findeth;
and unto whomsoever knocketh, it shall be opened.[3]

J have commanded that none of you should go away.[4]

*R*emember the worth of souls is great
   in the sight of God,
for the Lord your Redeemer suffered the pains of all.[5]

Assurances of
God's Compassion and Mercy

J have compassion upon you;
   my bowels are filled with mercy.[6]

---

1. 3 Ne. 9:14
2. 3 Ne. 12:45

3. 3 Ne. 14:8
4. 3 Ne. 18:25

5. D&C 18:10-11
6. 3 Ne. 17:7

*A*s I have sworn that the waters of Noah
    should no more go over the earth,
so have I sworn that I would not be wroth with thee.
    The mountains shall depart
and the hills be removed,
    but my kindness shall not depart from thee,
neither shall the covenant of my peace be removed,
    saith the Lord that hath mercy on thee.[1]

*R*emember how merciful
    the Lord hath been unto his children,
from the creation of Adam even down until this time,
    and ponder it in your heart.[2]

*R*emember, God is merciful;
    therefore, repent of that which thou hast done
which is contrary to the commandment
    which I gave you,
and thou art still called to the work.[3]

I do not condemn you;
    behold the wounds which pierced my side,
and also the prints of the nails
    in my hands and feet.[4]

---

1. 3 Ne. 22:9-10   3. D&C 3:10
2. Moro. 10:3   4. D&C 6:35, 37

Assurances of God's Forgiveness

$\mathcal{T}$hy sins are forgiven thee,
and thou shalt be blessed.[1]

※

$\mathcal{A}$s oft as you repent and seek forgiveness,
with real intent,
you are forgiven.[2]

※

$\mathcal{I}$, the Lord, cannot look upon sin
with the least degree of allowance;
nevertheless, all they who repent shall be forgiven.[3]

※

$\mathcal{T}$hou art not excusable in thy transgressions;
nevertheless, go thy way and sin no more.[4]

※

$\mathcal{Y}$ou sinned; nevertheless, I forgive you.[5]

※

$\mathcal{I}$nasmuch as you have
forgiven one another your trespasses,
even so I, the Lord, forgive you.[6]

※

$\mathcal{B}$ehold, your sins are forgiven you;
you are clean before me.
Therefore, lift up your head and rejoice.[7]

※

1. Enos 1:5
2. Moro. 6:8
3. D&C 1:31-32
4. D&C 24:2
5. D&C 75:8
6. D&C 82:1
7. D&C 110:5

*B*ehold, I have forgiven thee thy transgression;
>   by the Spirit ye are justified,
> and by the blood ye are sanctified.[1]

☞

Assurances of God's Acceptance

*B*lessed art thou,
>   because of the things which thou hast done.[2]

☞

*Y*ou shall be mine, saith the Lord of Hosts,
>   in that day when I make up my jewels;
> and I will spare you as a father spareth his own child.[3]

☞

*T*he weak things of the earth shall come forth
>   and break down the mighty and strong ones,
> that every one might speak
>   in the name of God the Lord,
> even the Savior of the world;
>   that my gospel might be proclaimed
> by the weak and simple unto the ends of the world,
>   and before kings and rulers.
> Behold, I am God, and have spoken it.[4]

☞

I do not condemn you;
>   go your way and perform the work
> which I have commanded you.[5]

☞

---

1. Moses 6:53, 60   3. 3 Ne. 24:17   5. D&C 6:35
2. 1 Ne. 2:1   4. D&C 1:19-20, 23-24

*Y*ou have been faithful over many things,
    and have done well.
Behold, I am merciful and will bless you,
    and you shall enter into the joy of these things.[1]

♞

*Y*e are they whom my Father hath given me;
    ye are my friends.[2]

♞

*B*lessed are ye—the Lord hath said it.[3]

♞

*L*et your soul be at rest
    concerning your spiritual standing.
Be more careful henceforth in observing your vows,
    and you shall be blessed
with exceedingly great blessings.[4]

♞

I, the Lord your God, am not displeased with you,
    notwithstanding your follies.[5]

♞

*T*here have been some few things with thee
    with which I, the Lord, was not well pleased.
Nevertheless, inasmuch as thou hast abased thyself
    thou shalt be exalted.
Therefore, all thy sins are forgiven thee;
    let thy heart be of good cheer before my face.[6]

♞

---

1. D&C 70:17-18   3. D&C 86:11   5. D&C 111:1
2. D&C 84:63   4. D&C 108:2-3   6. D&C 112:2-4

*W*hen you fall you shall rise again;
  therefore let no one despise my servant.[1]

〰

*Y*our prayers are acceptable before me.[2]

〰

*Y*e shall be great in mine eyes.[3]

〰

I have a work for thee.[4]

〰

*B*lessed art thou, for I have chosen thee,
  and thou shalt be made stronger
  than many waters;
and lo, I am with thee,
  even unto the end of thy days.[5]

〰

*T*hou wast chosen before thou wast born.[6]

〰

Assurances of God's Grace

*I*t is by grace that you are saved,
after all you can do.[7]

〰

---

1. D&C 117:13, 15   4. Moses 1:6   6. Abr. 3:23
2. D&C 124:2   5. Moses 1:25-26   7. 2 Ne. 25:23
3. D&C 124:13

*J*f ye come unto me
    I will show unto you your weakness;
and if ye humble yourselves before me,
    and have faith in me,
then will I make weak things
    become strong unto you.[1]

                ⁂

*B*ecause thou hast seen thy weakness,
    thou shalt be made strong.[2]

                ⁂

*T*hese commandments were given
    unto my servants in their weakness,
that inasmuch as they erred,
    they might be instructed,
and inasmuch as they were humble,
    they might be made strong.[3]

                ⁂

*M*y grace is sufficient for you;
    walk uprightly before me.[4]

                ⁂

J will be merciful unto your weakness.
    Therefore, be ye strong from henceforth; fear not.[5]

                ⁂

J will be merciful unto you;
    they who are weak among you
hereafter shall be made strong.[6]

                ⁂

---

1. Ether 12:27   3. D&C 1:24-26, 28 5. D&C 38:14-15
2. Ether 12:37   4. D&C 18:31   6. D&C 50:16

*B*ehold, ye are little children,
    and ye cannot bear all things now;
ye must grow in grace.[1]

☙

*B*ehold and hearken, saith the Lord your God,
    even Jesus Christ your advocate,
who knoweth your weakness,
    and how to succor them who are tempted:
Ye are blessed, for the angels rejoice over you,
    and your sins are forgiven you.[2]

☙

*Y*ou receive not of the fullness,
    but continue from grace to grace.[3]

☙

I will lift you up inasmuch
    as you will humble yourself before me;
I will give you grace and assurance
    wherewith you may stand.[4]

☙

*D*o all things that lie in your power;
    then may you stand still,
with the utmost assurance,
    for the arm of God to be revealed.[5]

☙

I will reward you
    according to the desire of your heart.[6]

☙

---

1. D&C 50:40   3. D&C 93:13.   5. D&C 123:17
2. D&C 62:1, 3   4. D&C 106:7-8.   6. D&C 137:9

Assurances of God's Support

*L*ook unto me, and ye shall live.[1]

O thou afflicted, tossed with tempest,
    and not comforted!
In righteousness shalt thou be established.[2]

*S*top and stand still until I command thee,
    and I will provide means
whereby thou mayest accomplish
    the thing which I have commanded thee.[3]

*S*tand fast in the work wherewith I have called you,
    and a hair of your head shall not be lost.[4]

*C*leave unto me.[5]

I myself will go with you and be in your midst,
    and nothing shall prevail against you.[6]

*T*he Lord shall be in your midst,
    and his glory shall be upon you.[7]

---

1. 3 Ne. 15:9
2. 3 Ne. 22:11, 14
3. D&C 5:34
4. D&C 9:14
5. D&C 11:19
6. D&C 32:3
7. D&C 45:59

I will go before you and be your rearward,
   and I will be in your midst;
you shall not be confounded.[1]

❧

*A*ll things shall work together for your good;
   you shall not be removed out of your place.[2]

❧

I will order all things for your good,
   as fast as ye are able to receive them.[3]

❧

I will bear you up as on eagle's wings.[4]

❧

Assurances of God's Protection

*T*he life of my servant shall be in my hand;
   I will go before you, and I will be your rearward.[5]

❧

*R*emember the promises which were made to you:
   that God would extend his arm and support you
against all the fiery darts of the adversary,
   and be with you in every time of trouble.[6]

❧

*B*ehold and lo, I am with you
   to bless you and deliver you forever.[7]

❧

---

1. D&C 49:27
2. D&C 90:24, 37
3. D&C 111:11
4. D&C 124:18
5. 3 Ne. 21:10, 29
6. D&C 3:5, 8
7. D&C 108:8

J am the Lord thy God,
  and will be with thee
even unto the end of the world
  and through all eternity.[1]

※

J am the Lord thy God;
  I dwell in heaven; the earth is my footstool;
I stretch my hand over the sea, and it obeys my voice.
  My name is Jehovah,
and my hand shall be over thee.[2]

※

Assurances of Divine Guidance

*C*ounsel with the Lord in all thy doings,
  and he will direct thee for good.[3]

※

J am the same that leadeth you to all good.[4]

※

*B*lessed art thou for what thou hast done;
  for thou hast inquired of me,
and behold, as often as thou hast inquired
  thou hast received instruction of my Spirit.
If it had not been so,
  thou wouldst not have come to the place
where thou art at this time.
  And now I tell thee these things
that thou mayest know
  that thou hast been enlightened
by the Spirit of truth.[5]

※

---

1. D&C 132:49   3. Alma 37:37   5. D&C 6:14-15
2. Abr. 2:7-8   4. Ether 4:12

Cast your mind upon the night
    that you cried unto me in your heart.
Did I not speak peace to your mind?
    What greater witness can you have?[1]

❧

Behold, you must study it out in your mind.
    Then ask me if it be right, and if it is right,
I will cause that you shall feel that it is right.[2]

❧

Go your way whithersoever I will,
    and it shall be given you by the Comforter
what you shall do and whither you shall go.[3]

❧

I will lead you whithersoever I will.[4]

❧

It shall be made known unto you what you shall do.[5]

❧

By my Spirit will I enlighten you,
    and by my power will I make known unto you
the secrets of my will.[6]

❧

Ye are little children,
    and ye cannot bear all things now;
nevertheless, be of good cheer,
    for I will lead you along.[7]

❧

---

1. D&C 6:22-23   4. D&C 38:33   6. D&C 76:10
2. D&C 9:8   5. D&C 52:4   7. D&C 78:17-18
3. D&C 31:11

J will send you the Comforter,
which shall teach you the way
whither you shall go.
Wherefore, fear not.[1]

❧

J will give unto the faithful
line upon line, precept upon precept.[2]

❧

*T*he Lord thy God shall lead thee by the hand,
and give thee answer to thy prayers.[3]

❧

*J*t shall be given you by the Holy Ghost
to know my will.[4]

❧

*B*ehold, I will lead thee by my hand.[5]

❧

Promises of Divine Inspiration

*R*eturn again, and prophesy
whatsoever things should come into your heart.[6]

❧

*J*t shall come to pass,
that if you shall ask the Father in my name,
you shall receive the Holy Ghost,
which giveth utterance,
that you may stand as a witness
of the things which you shall hear and see.[7]

❧

---

1. D&C 79:2, 4
2. D&C 98:12
3. D&C 112:10
4. D&C 124:5
5. Abr. 1:18
6. Hel. 13:3
7. D&C 14:8

*M*ake known thy calling before the world,
    and thy heart shall be opened to preach the truth.[1]

*O*pen your mouths and they shall be filled,
    and you shall become even as Nephi of old.
Yea, open your mouths and spare not,
    for lo, I am with you.[2]

*I*f thou shalt ask,
    thou shalt receive revelation upon revelation,
knowledge upon knowledge,
    that thou mayest know the peaceable things—
that which bringeth joy.[3]

*T*reasure up in your mind continually
    the words of life,
and it shall be given you in the very hour
    what ye shall say.[4]

*O*pen thy mouth, and it shall be filled,
    and I will give thee utterance;
for all flesh is in my hands,
    and I will do as seemeth me good.
Behold, my Spirit is upon you.[5]

---

1. D&C 23:2   3. D&C 42:61   5. Moses 6:32, 34
2. D&C 33:8-9   4. D&C 84:85

Promises of Divine Power

I will give you power.[1]

❧

Thou shalt have strength.[2]

❧

I will cause the heavens to shake for your good.[3]

❧

It shall come to pass that power shall rest upon thee;
I will be with thee and go before thy face.[4]

❧

Ye shall be endowed with power.[5]

❧

Ye who tremble shall be made strong,
and shall bring forth fruits of praise and wisdom.[6]

❧

You shall overcome all things.[7]

❧

Promises of Success in God's Work

Bear with patience thine afflictions,
and I will give unto you success.[8]

❧

---

1. D&C 5:13
2. D&C 24:7
3. D&C 35:24

4. D&C 39:12
5. D&C 43:16
6. D&C 52:17

7. D&C 76:60
8. Alma 26:27

*J*f ye have faith ye can do all things
which are expedient unto me.[1]

❧

*T*he works, and the designs, and the purposes of God
cannot be frustrated,
neither can they come to naught.
Remember, remember
that it is not the work of God that is frustrated,
but the work of the arm of flesh.[2]

❧

*D*oubt not, you shall do marvelous works.[3]

❧

I will cause you to bring forth as a very fruitful tree
which is planted in a goodly land,
by a pure stream,
that yieldeth much precious fruit.[4]

❧

---

1. Moro. 10:23   3. D&C 8:8
2. D&C 3:1, 3   4. D&C 97:9

Consolation and Comfort

Consolation for Those Who Feel Unsuccessful

*L*ift up your heads and be comforted,
    notwithstanding your many strugglings
which have been in vain.
    Lift up your heads and rejoice,
and put your trust in God.[1]

*B*lessed art thou; therefore,
    lift up thy head and rejoice,
for thou hast great cause to rejoice,
    for thou hast been faithful
in keeping the commandments of God.[2]

---

1. Mosiah 7:18-19   2. Alma 8:15

*B*lessed art thou,
 for I have beheld how thou hast
with unwearyingness sought my will.
 And now, because thou hast done this
with such unwearyingness,
 behold, I will bless thee forever.[1]

*A*ll things must come to pass in their time;
 wherefore, be not weary in well-doing,
for ye are laying the foundation of a great work,
 and out of small things proceedeth
that which is great.[2]

*Y*our offering is acceptable to me;
 I have seen your labor and toil for my name.[3]

I say unto you, that when any undertake
 to do a work in my name,
and go with all their might and with all they have
 to perform that work,
and cease not their diligence,
 but are hindered from performing it,
behold, it behooveth me to accept of their offerings.[4]

Especially for Missionaries

*I*f it so be that you should labor all your days
 and bring save it be one soul unto me,
how great shall be your joy![5]

---

1. Hel. 10:4-5   3. D&C 126:1-2   5. D&C 18:15
2. D&C 64:32-33   4. D&C 124:49

Especially for Parents

*Y*ou have had many afflictions
　　because of your family;
nevertheless, I will bless you and your family,
　　and the day cometh
that they will be one with you.[1]

Consolation for Those Who Feel Discouraged

*T*hou hast suffered afflictions and much sorrow.
　　Nevertheless, thou knowest the greatness of God,
and he shall consecrate thine afflictions for thy gain;
　　wherefore, thy soul shall be blessed.[2]

*L*ook unto God with firmness of mind,
　　and pray unto him with exceeding faith,
and he will console you in your afflictions.
　　Lift up your heads, and feast upon his love.[3]

*L*ift up your heads and be of good comfort,
　　for I know of the covenant
which ye have made unto me;
　　and I will covenant with my people,
that ye may know of a surety that I, the Lord God,
　　do visit my people in their afflictions.[4]

---

1. D&C 31:2　　　3. Jacob 3:1-2
2. 2 Ne. 2:1-3　　4. Mosiah 24:13-14

*L*ift up your head and be of good cheer;
for behold, the time is at hand
that I will fulfil all that which I have spoken.[1]

*B*e patient, for it is wisdom in me
that I have dealt with you after this manner.[2]

*R*ejoice evermore, and in everything give thanks,
     waiting patiently on the Lord;
for your prayers have entered in the ears
     of the Lord of Sabaoth,
and all things wherewith you have been afflicted
     shall work together for your good,
and to my name's glory.[3]

Especially for Missionaries

*B*e patient in long-suffering and afflictions,
that thou mayest show forth a good example in me,
and I will make an instrument of thee in my hands.[4]

---

1. 3 Ne. 1:13
2. D&C 9:3, 6

3. D&C 98:1-3
4. Alma 17:11

Consolation for Those Who Feel Abandoned

Zion hath said:
> The Lord hath forsaken me,
> my Lord hath forgotten me—
> but I will show that I hath not.
> Behold, I have engraven thee
> upon the palms of my hands.[1]

❧

Be patient in afflictions, for thou shalt have many;
> but lo, I am with thee,
> even unto the end of thy days.[2]

❧

Lift up your hearts and be glad,
> for I am in your midst.[3]

❧

What I say unto one, I say unto all:
> Be of good cheer, little children,
> for I am in your midst,
> and I have not forsaken you.[4]

❧

Behold and lo, mine eyes are upon you,
> whose prayers I have heard, whose heart I know,
> and whose desires have come up before me.[5]

❧

I will be with you even unto the end.[6]

❧

---

1. 1 Ne. 21:14, 16
2. D&C 24:8
3. D&C 29:5
4. D&C 61:36
5. D&C 67:1-2
6. D&C 75:13

*P*eace be with you;
    my blessings continue with you.[1]

ॐ

I will be on your right hand and on your left,
    and my Spirit shall be in your heart,
and mine angels round about you, to bear you up.[2]

ॐ

*B*ehold, my Spirit is upon you,
    and thou shalt abide in me, and I in you.[3]

ॐ

Consolation for Those Who Grieve

*T*he Lord will comfort Zion,
    he will comfort all her waste places.
Joy and gladness shall be found therein,
    thanksgiving and the voice of melody.[4]

ॐ

I am he; yea, I am he that comforteth you.[5]

ॐ

*T*he Lord shall give thee rest from thy sorrow.[6]

ॐ

*B*e comforted.[7]

ॐ

---

1. D&C 82:23   4. 2 Ne. 8:3   6. 2 Ne. 24:3
2. D&C 84:88   5. 2 Ne. 8:12   7. Alma 17:10
3. Moses 6:34

*B*lessed are all they that mourn,
    for they shall be comforted.[1]

*U*nto you shall the Son of Righteousness arise
    with healing in his wings.[2]

I will encircle thee in the arms of my love.
    I am the light which shineth in darkness.[3]

*Y*ou shall have peace in me.[4]

*Y*our weeping I have seen,
    and I will cause that you shall mourn no longer.[5]

*T*hou hast seen great sorrow;
    but behold, the days of thy deliverance are come,
and you shall receive a blessing
    so great as you never have known.[6]

*T*hou shalt live together in love,
    insomuch that thou shalt weep for the loss
of them that die.[7]

---

1. 3 Ne. 12:4   4. D&C 19:23   6. D&C 39:9-10
2. 3 Ne. 25:2   5. D&C 21:8   7. D&C 42:45
3. D&C 6:20-21

Let your heart be comforted;
　　for behold and lo,
I am with you even unto the end.[1]

❧

Peace be unto thy soul.[2]

❧

Comfort for Those Who Are Afraid

I am the Lord thy God, whose waves roar;
　　I have covered thee in the shadow of mine hand.[3]

❧

Fear not. I am God,
　　and I am with you.[4]

❧

Thou shalt be far from oppression
　　for thou shalt not fear,
and from terror for it shall not come near thee.[5]

❧

I am in the midst of you. Therefore, fear not.[6]

❧

Fear not, little children,
　　for you are mine, and I have overcome.
You are of them that my Father hath given me,
　　and none of them that my Father hath given me
shall be lost.[7]

❧

---

1. D&C 100:12, 15
2. D&C 121:7
3. 2 Ne. 8:15-16
4. Hel. 5:26; 8:23
5. 3 Ne. 22:14
6. D&C 6:32, 34
7. D&C 50:41-42

*B*e of good cheer, and do not fear,
    for I the Lord am with you,
and will stand by you.[1]

※

*M*y friends, fear not;
    let your hearts be comforted.[2]

※

*F*ear not even death;
    for in this world your joy is not full,
but in me your joy is full.[3]

※

*H*old on thy way; fear not,
    for God shall be with you forever and ever.[4]

※

Comfort for Those Who Worry

*P*eace, peace be unto you.[5]

※

*L*ook unto me in every thought;
    doubt not, fear not.[6]

※

*T*hou needst not fear;
    wherefore, lift up thy heart and rejoice.[7]

※

---

1. D&C 68:6
2. D&C 98:1
3. D&C 101:36
4. D&C 122:9
5. Hel. 5:47
6. D&C 6:36
7. D&C 25:9, 13

*B*e not troubled.[1]

❧

*T*here are many dangers;
　　nevertheless, all flesh is in mine hand.[2]

❧

*L*et your heart be glad, and fear not,
　　saith your Lord Jesus Christ.[3]

❧

*Y*our families are well;
　　they are in mine hands,
and in me there is all power.[4]

❧

*B*e still and know that I am God.[5]

❧

For Times of Conflict

*Y*ou shall hear of wars, and rumors of wars;
　　see that ye be not troubled.[6]

❧

---

1. D&C 45:35　　　3. D&C 79:4　　　5. D&C 101:16
2. D&C 61:4, 6　　4. D&C 100:1　　6. JS-M 1:23

Testimony and Trust

Testimonies that God Hears Our Prayers

J know that God will give liberally to him that asketh.
    Yea, my God will give me;
therefore I will lift up my voice.[1]

*H*is glory shall be the glory of the
    Only Begotten of the Father,
full of grace, equity, and truth,
    full of patience, mercy, and long-suffering,
quick to hear the cries of his people
    and to answer their prayers.[2]

*T*he Lord is merciful unto all
    who will, in the sincerity of their hearts,
call upon his holy name.[3]

*T*hey who seek God shall find him,
    and shall not be forsaken.[4]

---

1. 2 Ne. 4:35   3. Hel. 3:27   4. D&C 88:83
2. Alma 9:26

I will not cease to call upon God.[1]

❧

I lifted up my voice unto the Lord my God,
   and the Lord hearkened and heard me.[2]

❧

I found the testimony of James to be true—
   that any who lack wisdom might ask of God,
and obtain, and not be upbraided.[3]

❧

Testimonies that God Is Always Near

*H*ow merciful is our God unto us,
   for he stretches forth his hands all the day long.
Wherefore, cleave unto God as he cleaveth unto you.[4]

❧

*T*hou art merciful, O God,
   for thou hast heard my prayer,
even when I was in the wilderness.[5]

❧

*H*e comprehendeth all things,
   and all things are before him,
and all things are round about him;
   he is above all things,
and in all things,
   and through all things,
and round about all things,
   forever and ever.[6]

❧

---

1. Moses 1:18	3. JS-H 1:26	5. Alma 33:4
2. Abr. 1:15	4. Jacob 6:4-5	6. D&C 88:41

Testimonies that God Comforts Us

Mine eyes water my pillow by night,
  and I cry unto my God in faith,
and I know that he will hear my cry.[1]

❧

When our hearts were depressed,
  and we were about to turn back,
behold, the Lord comforted us.[2]

❧

I did cry unto God
  and did find peace to my soul.[3]

❧

My heart has been filled with sorrow;
  nevertheless, I know that I shall be lifted up.[4]

❧

All they who have mourned shall be comforted.[5]

❧

If thou art sorrowful,
  call on the Lord thy God with supplication.[6]

❧

Enoch wept, and said unto the heavens:
  I will refuse to be comforted.
But the Lord said unto Enoch:
  Lift up your heart, and be glad.[7]

❧

---

1. 2 Ne. 33:3   4. Morm. 2:19   6. D&C 136:29
2. Alma 26:27   5. D&C 101:14   7. Moses 7:44
3. Alma 38:8

Testimonies that God Shares Our Sorrows

Surely he has borne our griefs,
   and carried our sorrows.[1]

※

The Son of God shall go forth,
   suffering pains and afflictions of every kind;
he will take upon him the pains
   and sicknesses of his people,
and he will take upon him their infirmities,
   that he may know according to the flesh
how to succor his people
   according to their infirmities.[2]

※

In all your afflictions he is afflicted.[3]

※

And it came to pass that the God of heaven wept.[4]

※

Testimonies that We Need Not Fear

Behold, God is my salvation;
   I will trust, and not be afraid,
for the Lord Jehovah
   is my strength and my song.[5]

※

---

1. Mosiah 14:4   3. D&C 133:53   5. 2 Ne. 22:2
2. Alma 7:11-12   4. Moses 7:28

*H*e is the light and the life of the world;
    yea, a light that is endless,
that can never be darkened;
    yea, a life which is endless,
that there can be no more death.[1]

⁂

*A*nd it came to pass that
    Moses began to fear exceedingly;
nevertheless, calling upon God, he received strength.[2]

⁂

Expressions of Trust in God's Will

I said, I have labored in vain,
    I have spent my strength for naught;
surely my judgment is with the Lord,
    and my work with my God.[3]

⁂

*C*heer up your hearts,
    and reconcile yourselves to the will of God.[4]

⁂

*T*hy will, O Lord, be done, and not mine.[5]

⁂

*T*he Lord worketh in me to do according to his will.[6]

⁂

---

1. Mosiah 16:9   3. 1 Ne. 21:4   5. Jacob 7:14
2. Moses 1:20   4. 2 Ne. 10:23-24   6. W of M 1:7

O Lord, thy righteous will be done;
    for I remember that thou hast said
that thou hast loved the world
    even unto the laying down of thy life.[1]

❧

*L*et God rule according to the counsel of his own will.[2]

❧

*L*et your heart be comforted,
    for all things shall work together for your good.[3]

❧

*T*he servant said unto his lord:
    When shall these things be?
And he said unto his servant: When I will;
    go ye straightway and do all things
whatsoever I have commanded you.
    And his servant went straightway
and did all things
    whatsoever his lord commanded him,
and after many days all things were fulfilled.[4]

❧

*F*ather, thy will be done.[5]

❧

For Those Facing the Possibility of Death

*I*f I die, let me die unto thee,
    and if I live, let me live unto thee.[6]

❧

---

1. Ether 12:29, 33   3. D&C 100:15   5. Moses 4:2
2. D&C 58:20   4. D&C 101:59-60, 62   6. D&C 42:44

Expressions of Trust Despite Uncertainty

I am led by the Spirit,
   not knowing beforehand
the things which I shall do.[1]

≫

*T*he Lord hath commanded me for a wise purpose,
   which purpose I know not.
But the Lord knoweth all things from the beginning;
   wherefore, he prepareth a way
to accomplish all his works.[2]

≫

*H*ow unsearchable are the depths
   of the mysteries of the Lord;
it is impossible that we should find out all his ways.[3]

≫

I do this, for thus it whispereth me
   according to the workings of the Spirit,
which is in me.
   And now, I do not know all things,
but the Lord knoweth all things which are to come;
   wherefore he worketh in me
to do according to his will.[4]

≫

*I*f the Lord saith unto us go, we will go.[5]

≫

---

1. 1 Ne. 4:6   3. Jacob 4:8   5. Alma 27:8
2. 1 Ne. 9:5-6   4. W of M 1:7

Reflections on Desire

The Spirit said unto me:
    Behold, what desirest thou?[1]

※

I will grant unto thee according to thy desires,
    because of thy faith.[2]

※

God granteth unto all according to their desire.[3]

※

O Lord, thou hast given us a commandment,
    that we must call upon thee,
that from thee we may receive
    according to our desires.[4]

※

If ye have desires to serve God,
    ye are called to the work.[5]

※

Even as you desire of me
    so it shall be unto you;
if you desire, you shall be the means
    of doing much good in this generation.[6]

※

I have spoken unto thee because of thy desires.[7]

※

---

1. 1 Ne. 11:2
2. Enos 1:12
3. Alma 29:4

4. Ether 3:2
5. D&C 4:3

6. D&C 6:8
7. D&C 6:20

*W*hat desirest thou?
  For if you ask what you will,
it shall be granted unto you.[1]

❧

*Y*e shall both have according to your desires,
  for ye both joy in that which ye have desired.[2]

❧

*T*rifle not with these things;
  do not ask for that which you ought not.[3]

❧

*B*ehold, according to your desires,
  yea, even according to your faith,
shall it be done unto you.[4]

❧

I, the Lord, will judge all
  according to the desire of their hearts.[5]

❧

Reflections for Perfectionists

*I*f I err, I excuse myself,
  because of the weakness which is in me.[6]

❧

---

1. D&C 7:1	3. D&C 8:10	5. D&C 137:9
2. D&C 7:8	4. D&C 11:17	6. 1 Ne. 19:6

My hearth sorroweth because of my flesh;
    my soul grieveth because of mine iniquities.
I am encompassed about,
    because of the temptations and sins
which do so easily beset me.
    Nevertheless, I know in whom I have trusted;
my God hath been my support.[1]

How great the importance
    to make these things known,
that there is no flesh
    that can dwell in the presence of God,
save it be through the merits, and mercy, and grace
    of the Holy Messiah.[2]

It is by grace that we are saved, after all we can do.[3]

The Lord God showeth unto us our weakness
    that we may know that it is by his grace
that we have power.[4]

By small and simple things
    are great things brought to pass.
The Lord God doth work by very small means
    to bring about his great and eternal purposes.[5]

---

1. 2 Ne. 4:17-20   3. 2 Ne. 25:23   5. Alma 37:6-7
2. 2 Ne. 2:8   4. Jacob 4:7

*C*ome unto Christ, and be perfected in him;
 and if ye deny yourselves of all ungodliness,
and love God with all your might, mind, and strength,
 then is his grace sufficient for you,
that ye become holy, without spot.[1]

*L*et no one count these as small things;
 for there is much which lieth in futurity
which depends upon these things.[2]

*B*lessed be the name of God,
 for because of my transgression
my eyes are opened.[3]

*N*o one need suppose me guilty
 of any great or malignant sins.
A disposition to commit such was never in my nature.
 But I often felt condemned
for my weakness and imperfections;
 therefore I betook myself
to prayer and supplication.[4]

---

1. Moro. 10:32-33 3. Moses 5:10
2. D&C 123:15   4. JS-H 1:28-29

Reflections for Those Called To Serve

Use boldness, but not overbearance,
    that ye may be filled with love.
Do not say: O God, I thank thee
    that we are better than these;
but rather acknowledge your unworthiness
    before God at all times.[1]

⁂

The remission of sins bringeth meekness
    and lowliness of heart;
and because of meekness and lowliness of heart
    cometh the visitation of the Holy Ghost,
which Comforter filleth with hope and perfect love,
    which love endureth by diligence unto prayer,
until the end shall come,
    when all the saints shall dwell with God.[2]

⁂

You cannot assist in this work
    except you shall be humble and full of love,
being temperate in all things.[3]

⁂

Succor the weak,
    lift up the hands which hang down,
strengthen the feeble knees.[4]

⁂

---

1. Alma 38:12, 14   3. D&C 12:8
2. Moro. 8:26   4. D&C 81:5

The powers of heaven cannot be handled
    except by persuasion, by long-suffering,
by gentleness and meekness,
    by love unfeigned, by kindness without hypocrisy,
showing forth that thy love and faithfulness
    are stronger than the cords of death.[1]

Reflections for Those Who Feel Overwhelmed

I know that the Lord shall prepare a way.[2]

Let us be strong like unto Moses;
    for he spake unto the waters of the Red Sea
and they divided hither and thither,
    and our forebears came through on dry ground.[3]

The Lord is able to do all things
    according to his will for us.[4]

Ye have not come this far
    save it were by the word of Christ,
relying wholly upon the merits
    of him who is mighty to save.
Wherefore, press forward
    with a steadfastness in Christ,
having a perfect brightness of hope.[5]

1. D&C 121:36, 41-44   3. 1 Ne. 4:2   5. 2 Ne. 31:19-20
2. 1 Ne. 3:7   4. 1 Ne. 7:12

*W*hoso believeth in God
    might with surety hope for a better world,
which hope maketh an anchor to our souls,
    making us sure and steadfast.[1]

⁊℃

*L*et all things be done in order,
    not in haste, nor by flight,
according to the knowledge
    which you receive from time to time.[2]

⁊℃

*L*et the morrow take thought for the things of itself.[3]

⁊℃

Reflections for Those Who Feel Weary

*I*t is not requisite that you should run
    faster than you have strength.[4]

⁊℃

I know that whosoever shall put their trust in God
    shall be supported in their trials,
and their troubles, and their afflictions.[5]

⁊℃

*C*ry unto God for all thy support.[6]

⁊℃

I am but mortal,
    and I have but the strength of a mortal body.[7]

⁊℃

---

1. Ether 12:4   4. Mosiah 4:27   6. Alma 37:36
2. D&C 58:55-56   5. Alma 36:3   7. Moro. 9:18
3. D&C 84:84

$\mathcal{D}$o not run faster or labor more
than you have strength and means provided you.[1]

$\mathcal{S}$eek not to be cumbered.[2]

Reflections for Those Who Feel Uncertain

$\mathcal{I}$ do not know the meaning of all things;
nevertheless, I know that God loveth his children.[3]

$\mathcal{F}$aith is not to have a perfect knowledge of things;
therefore, if ye have faith
ye hope for things which are not seen.[4]

$\mathcal{E}$ven if ye can no more than desire to believe,
let this desire work in you,
until it beginneth to enlarge your soul,
yea, to enlighten your understanding.[5]

$\mathcal{F}$aith is things which are hoped for and not seen.[6]

---

1. D&C 10:4
2. D&C 66:10
3. 1 Ne. 11:17
4. Alma 32:21
5. Alma 32:27-28
6. Ether 12:6

*Y*ou have not understood;
    you have supposed that I would give unto you,
when you took no thought save to ask me.
    But behold, you must study it out in your mind.[1]

❧

*Y*ou are left to inquire for yourself
    and ponder upon the things
which you have received.[2]

❧

*G*ive heed to that which is written,
    and pray always that I may unfold the same
to your understanding.[3]

❧

Y cannot behold, for the present time,
    the design of your God
concerning those things which shall come hereafter,
    and the glory which shall follow.[4]

❧

*I*t is not meet that I should command in all things.
    Wherefore, you should be anxiously engaged
    in a good cause,
and do many things of your own free will,
    and bring to pass much righteousness;
for the power is in you,
    whereby you are an agent unto yourself.[5]

❧

*Y*ou may do as seemeth you good,
    it mattereth not unto me; only be faithful.[6]

❧

---

1. D&C 9:7-8   3. D&C 32:4   5. D&C 58:26-28
2. D&C 30:3   4. D&C 58:3   6. D&C 62:5

*T*he day shall come when you shall comprehend.[1]

I, the Lord, have put forth my hand
 to exert the powers of heaven;
ye cannot see it now,
 yet a little while and ye shall see it,
and know that I am.[2]

*W*e believe that God will yet reveal many things.[3]

Reflections for Those Who Feel Rejected or Humiliated

*T*he Lord God will help me,
 therefore shall I not be confounded.
Therefore have I set my face like a flint,
 and I know that I shall not be ashamed.[4]

*W*ho art thou,
 that thou shouldst be afraid of the arm of flesh,
which shall be made like unto grass?[5]

*H*e is despised and rejected;
 a man of sorrows, and acquainted with grief.[6]

---

1. D&C 88:49   3. A of F 1:9   5. 2 Ne. 8:12
2. D&C 84:119   4. 2 Ne. 7:7   6. Mosiah 14:3

Thou hast heard me when I have been cast out
 and have been despised by mine enemies;
yea, thou didst hear my cries.
 Thou wast merciful when I prayed
concerning those who were mine enemies,
 and thou didst turn them to me.[1]

※

Fear not, for thou shalt not be ashamed,
 neither be thou confounded,
for thou shalt not be put to shame.
 For thy maker, the Lord of hosts is his name;
and thy Redeemer, the Holy One of Israel.[2]

※

Fools mock,
 but my grace is sufficient for the meek,
and they shall take no advantage of your weakness.[3]

※

I am Jesus Christ, the Son of God.
 I came unto mine own,
and mine own received me not.[4]

※

Trust in me,
 reviling not against revilers.[5]

※

I call upon the weak things of the world,
 those who are unlearned and despised,
to reprove the nations by the power of my Spirit.
 Their arm shall be my arm,
and I will be their shield and their buckler.[6]

※

1. Alma 33:4, 10 3. Ether 12:26 5. D&C 19:30
2. 3 Ne. 22:4-5   4. D&C 10:57   6. D&C 35:13-14

$\mathcal{T}$rust in me and ye shall not be confounded.[1]

Reflections for Those Who Feel Anxious About Speaking or Testifying

$\mathcal{J}$ speak with boldness,
   having authority from God;
and I fear not what flesh can do,
   for perfect love casteth out all fear.
And I am filled with charity,
   which is everlasting love.[2]

$\mathcal{J}$ speak boldly; God hath commanded me.[3]

$\mathcal{F}$irst seek to obtain my word,
   and then shall your tongue be loosed;
then, if you desire,
   you shall have my Spirit and my word.[4]

$\mathcal{O}$pen your mouth in my cause,
   not fearing what flesh can do,
for I am with you.[5]

---

1. D&C 84:116
2. Moro. 8:16-17

3. Moro. 8:21
4. D&C 11:21

5. D&C 30:11

*S*peak the thoughts that I shall put into your heart,
   and you shall not be confounded;
but declare whatsoever thing ye declare
   in solemnity of heart, in the spirit of meekness.[1]

※

---

1. D&C 100:5, 7

Section 3

The Joy of Service

The joy we receive from the Spirit impels us to reach out in service to others. Latter-day Saints offer service in various arenas. We serve the members of our own families as we work with them to build a home life that invites the sanctifying presence of the Holy Spirit of promise. We serve other individuals and families around us as we magnify callings as home and visiting teachers. We serve our local faith communities as we accept Church callings of various kinds: musician, teacher, youth leader, advisor, coordinator, committee member, groundskeeper.

Even those who render pastoral care in the Church—Primary and Relief Society presidencies, bishoprics, high councils, stake presidencies, and so on—do so without remuneration and in addition to the usual obligations of family and work, while missionaries accept the call to build up the Church throughout the world for periods of eighteen months to two years, at their own expense.

We serve the Church with our means as we contribute our tithing, fast-offerings, and other free-will contributions. We serve even the dead as we perform gospel ordinances such as baptism, vicariously, on their behalf in the temples.

"To serve," Spencer W. Kimball taught, is "to succor those in need of succor," adding that "the measure of our love for our fellowman and, in a large sense, the measure of our love for the Lord, is what we do for one another and for the poor and distressed."[1] People who have experienced the goodness of God in their lives cannot help but be scandalized by what Gordon B. Hinckley has denounced as "the deplorable conditions that we see of civil war and conflict and all of the problems of hunger and strife and poverty across the world."[2] We cannot fail to recognize that the God whose love we have experienced intends better for his children than a world where

1. *Ensign,* Nov. 1977, p. 77.
2. *Ensign,* Dec. 1995, p. 66.

millions go hungry because too much food is wasted by those who don't need it, while not enough finds its way into the pots of those who do; a world where children still suffer from diseases for which vaccines or treatment have been available for decades to those living in the more affluent countries; a world where centuries-old rivalries and hatreds erupt into terrorism, war, and campaigns of ethnic cleansing or genocide; a world, sizeable portions of which are ruled by corrupt or repressive governments; a world, LDS scholars warn, where our own "reckless disregard for the natural environment" threatens to bring about the fulfillment of prophecies that describe the earth as "cursed" and "utterly wasted."[3]

Clearly, the human family has failed to properly discharge its stewardship of the earth and its bounty. In the face of such enormous problems, it is tempting to "throw up our hands and do nothing but pray for the end to come so the millennial reign can begin." But, Glenn L. Pace has cautioned, "to do so would forfeit our right to participate in the grand scene we are all awaiting."[4] As professed disciples of Christ, we find ourselves under an "admonition to be anxiously engaged or actively involved in good causes in the Church and in [our] neighborhoods, communities, and even throughout the world,"[5] adding our widow's mite, as it were, to the on-going efforts of like-minded people on behalf of our needy brothers and sisters. The Lord calls us to action, to service, to consecration, to stewardship. In the scriptures, God calls upon his children everywhere to embrace his gospel as "the answer to all the problems of the world."[6] He calls us, as individuals and as nations, to work for unity and peace, equality and justice, to impart of our substance for the aid of the poor, to reject what President Kimball called "the

3. Alan J. Hawkins *et al., BYU Studies*, Winter 1993, p. 285.
4. *Ensign*, Nov. 1990, p. 8.
5. Howard W. Hunter, *Ensign*, Nov. 1992, p. 96.
6. Spencer W. Kimball, *Ensign*, Nov. 1974, p. 119.

heedless . . . pursuit of materialism,"[7] to take the steps necessary to prevent our own destruction.

However bleak our situation may seem, our experience of the greatness of God gives us faith that, in fact, the situation is far from hopeless. God has promised that if we live in accordance with his teachings, we will be delivered—that at the last, God will cause us to inherit a better world—and we know that his promises cannot fail. Jeffrey R. Holland has testified:

> I . . . know that the gospel of Jesus Christ holds the answer to every social and political and economic problem this world has ever faced. And I know we can each do something, however small that act may seem to be. We can pay an honest tithe and give our fast and freewill offerings according to our own circumstances. And we can watch for other ways to help. To worthy causes and needy people, we can give time if we don't have money, and we can give love when our time runs out. We can share the loaves we have and trust God that the cruse of oil will not fail.[8]

There is much discussion among Christians about how to respond to our world's many problems in light of the teachings of Jesus. Latter-day Saints have much to contribute to that discussion. We come from a heritage of "ordinary men and women, plain spoken, hard working, but made noble because they shared a vision, a vision of a different world, a world where injustice and oppression, poverty and ignorance would be dispelled and a world where men and women would be brothers and sisters."[9] In our faith tradition, that vision is called Zion. The building up of Zion through Christlike service to our fellow beings, whether at home or abroad, has been one of the chief objects of the Restoration from the days of Joseph Smith to the present—one of our chief objects, and one of our chief joys.

---

7. *Ensign*, Oct. 1985, p. 4.
8. *Ensign*, May 1996, p. 31.
9. Alexander B. Morrison, *Church News*, 14 Oct. 1995, p. 4.

Calls to Serve Our Fellow Beings

Calls to Action

*W*o be unto they who are at ease in Zion!
Wo be unto they who cry: All is well![1]

*D*o you suppose that the Lord will deliver us,
while we sit and do not make use of the means
which the Lord has provided for us?[2]

*I*t is not meet that I should command in all things;
for one that is compelled in all things
is a slothful and not a wise servant.
Wherefore, you should be anxiously engaged
in a good cause,
and do many things of your own free will,
and bring to pass much righteousness;
for the power is in you,
wherein you are agents unto yourselves.[3]

---

1. 2 Ne. 28:24-25   2. Alma 60:21   3. D&C 58:26-28

*A*ll victory and glory is brought to pass unto you
through your diligence, faithfulness,
and prayers of faith.[1]

*G*o thy way and do as I have told you;
and fear not,
for no one shall have power to stop my work.[2]

Calls to Service

*W*hen ye are in the service of your fellow beings
ye are in the service of your God.[3]

*N*ow, as ye are desirous to be called God's people—
are ye willing to bear one another's burdens,
that they may be light?
Yea, are ye willing to mourn
with those that mourn,
and comfort those that stand in need of comfort?[4]

*L*et each of you seek the interest of your neighbor,
doing all things with an eye single
to the glory of God.[5]

---

1. D&C 103:36   3. Mosiah 2:17   5. D&C 82:19
2. D&C 136:17   4. Mosiah 18:8-9

J speak concerning my afflicted people:
    There are many who will say, Where is their God?
Let him deliver them in their time of trouble;
    we will not go up and will keep our moneys.
I say unto you, such have not learned
    to impart of their substance, as becometh saints.[1]

❧

*S*trengthen your brothers and sisters
    in all your conversation,
in all your prayers,
    in all your exhortations,
and in all your doings.[2]

❧

*L*ift up your voice loud and long,
    in the midst of the people,
to plead the cause of the poor and needy,
    and I will accept of your offerings.[3]

❧

*T*hus saith the Lord:
    I am angry with this people,
for their hearts have waxed hard,
    and their ears are dull of hearing,
and their eyes cannot see afar off.[4]

❧

---

1. D&C 105:1, 3, 5   3. D&C 124:75
2. D&C 108:7   4. Moses 6:27

Calls to Consecration

Ye must not perform any thing unto the Lord
save in the first place ye shall
pray unto the Father,
in the name of Christ,
that he will consecrate thy performance.[1]

❦

Come unto Christ, and
offer your whole souls as an offering unto him.[2]

❦

Serve him who has created you,
and is preserving you from day to day
by lending you breath,
even supporting you from one moment
to another—
I say, serve him with all your souls,
for he hath created you
and granted unto you your lives,
for which ye are indebted to him.[3]

❦

Ye are eternally indebted to your heavenly Father,
to render to him all that you have and are.[4]

❦

Come unto Christ,
and love God with all your might,
mind, and strength.[5]

❦

---

1. 2 Ne. 32:9   3. Mosiah 2:21, 23   5. Moro. 10:32
2. Omni 1:26   4. Mosiah 2:34

*B*ehold, a marvelous work is about to come forth
    among the inhabitants of the earth.
Therefore, O ye that embark in the service of God,
    see that serve him
with all your heart, might, mind, and strength.[1]

*C*leave unto me with all your heart,
    that you may assist in bringing to pass
those things of which has been spoken.[2]

*Y*our whole labor shall be in Zion,
    with all your soul, from henceforth.[3]

*I*f ye labor with all your might,
    I will consecrate that wherein ye labor
that it shall be made holy.[4]

Calls to Stewardship

*Y*e were created of the dust of the earth,
    but behold, it belongeth to him who created you.[5]

---

1. D&C 4:1-2   3. D&C 30:11   5. Mosiah 2:25
2. D&C 11:19   4. D&C 124:44

*A*ll things which come of the earth,
    in the season thereof,
are made for the benefit
    and the use of the whole human family.
And it pleaseth God
    that he hath given these things unto us,
for unto this end were they made to be used—
    with judgment, not to excess, neither by extortion.[1]

*R*emember that your stewardship
    will I require at your hands.[2]

*T*hou shalt be diligent in preserving what thou hast,
    that thou mayest be a wise steward;
for it is the gift of the Lord thy God,
    and thou art his steward.[3]

*R*eplenish the earth, and subdue it,
    and have dominion over the fish of the sea,
and over the fowl of the air,
    and over every living thing
that moveth upon the earth.[4]

Calls for Unity

*B*e determined in one mind and in one heart,
    united in all things.[5]

---

1. D&C 59:18, 20   3. D&C 136:27   5. 2 Ne. 1:21
2. D&C 124:14   4. Moses 2:28

*T*hose of you which have persecuted your neighbor—
    do ye not suppose that such things
are abominable unto him who created all flesh?
    And the one being is as precious in his sight
    as the other.[1]

୨୦

*L*et there be no contention one with another,
    but look forward with one eye,
having your hearts knit together in unity
    and in love one towards another;
and thus you shall become the children of God.[2]

୨୦

*L*ove your enemies, bless them that curse you,
    do good to them that hate you,
and pray for them
    who despitefully use you and persecute you,
that you may be the children
    of your Father in heaven,
who maketh his sun to rise
    on the evil and on the good.[3]

୨୦

I say unto you: Be one,
    and if ye are not one, ye are not mine.[4]

୨୦

O ye nations of the earth,
    how often would I have gathered you
as a hen gathereth her chicks under her wings![5]

୨୦

---

1. Jacob 2:20-21   3. 3 Ne. 12:44-45   5. D&C 43:24
2. Mosiah 18:21-22   4. D&C 38:27

*B*ehold these thy fellow beings;
　　they are the workmanship of mine own hands.
Therefore, I have given commandment
　　that they should love one another.[1]

Calls for Peace

*W*hoso shall publish peace,
　　how beautiful shall they be.[2]

*L*et there be no persecutions among you,
　　that there may be an equality among all people,
and let no pride nor haughtiness disturb your peace.[3]

*L*et us be wise and do that
　　which will make for the peace of this people.[4]

*L*et us bury our weapons of war, for peace.[5]

*B*lessed are all the peacemakers,
　　for they shall be called the children of God.[6]

---

1. Moses 7:32-33　　3. Mosiah 27:3-4　　5. Alma 24:19
2. 1 Ne. 13:37　　　4. Mosiah 29:10　　6. 3 Ne. 12:9

J remember the word of God which saith
    that if their works be good,
then they are good also.
    And now I judge this of you
because of your peaceable walk
    with the inhabitants of the earth.[1]

❧

*R*enounce war and proclaim peace.[2]

❧

*S*ue for peace to all people:
    lift up an ensign of peace,
make a proclamation of peace
    unto the ends of the earth,
and make proposals for peace
    unto those who have smitten you,
according to the voice of the Spirit
    which is in you.[3]

❧

*C*ease to contend one with another;
    cease to speak evil one of another.[4]

❧

Calls for Equality and Justice

*W*o unto them that decree unrighteous decrees,
    to turn away the needy from judgment,
and to take away the right
    from the poor of my people![5]

❧

---

1. Moro. 7:4-5   3. D&C 105:38-40   5. 2 Ne. 20:1-2
2. D&C 98:16   4. D&C 136:23

J desire that inequality should be no more,
  but that all may enjoy their rights
and privileges alike.[1]

⁂

*D*eal justly,
  and you shall have justice restored unto you.[2]

⁂

*E*steem your neighbor as yourself,
  and practice virtue and holiness before me.
Again I say unto you:
  esteem your neighbor as yourself.[3]

⁂

*W*hat man among you, having twelve sons,
  saith unto the one,
Be thou clothed in robes and sit thou here,
  and to the other,
Be thou clothed in rags and sit thou there,
  and looketh upon his sons and saith, I am just?[4]

⁂

*B*ehold, the beasts of the field and the fowls of the air,
  and that which cometh of the earth,
is ordained for the use of the whole human family,
  for food and for raiment,
that you might have in abundance.
  But it is not given that one person
should possess that which is above another;
  wherefore the world lieth in sin.[5]

⁂

---

1. Mosiah 29:32   3. D&C 38:24-25   5. D&C 49:19-20
2. Alma 41:14   4. D&C 38:26

*I*n your temporal things you shall be equal,
    and this not grudgingly;
otherwise the abundance of the
    manifestations of the Spirit
shall be withheld.[1]

               ❧

*I*f ye are not equal in earthly things,
    ye cannot be equal in obtaining heavenly things.[2]

               ❧

*L*et one speak at a time,
    and let all listen to that one's sayings,
that when all have spoken, all may be edified of all
    and everyone may have an equal privilege.[3]

               ❧

*T*hat law of the land which is constitutional,
    supporting the principle of freedom
in maintaining rights and privileges,
    belongs to all mankind
and is justifiable before me.[4]

               ❧

*T*he laws and constitution of the people
    should be maintained
for the rights and protection of all flesh,
    according to just principles.[5]

               ❧

*B*y thy word many high ones shall be made low,
    and by thy word many low ones shall be lifted up.[6]

               ❧

---

1. D&C 70:14   3. D&C 88:122   5. D&C 101:77
2. D&C 78:6   4. D&C 98:5   6. D&C 112:8

*B*e not partial towards thy brothers and sisters
    in love,
but let thy love be for them as for thyself,
    and let thy love abound unto all.[1]

Calls to Aid the Poor

*B*e familiar with all and free with your substance,
    that they may be rich like unto you.[2]

*I*f ye seek for riches,
    seek them for the intent to do good:
to clothe the naked,
    and to feed the hungry,
and to liberate the captive
    and administer relief to the sick and the afflicted.[3]

*S*uccor those that stand in need of your succor;
    administer of your substance
unto those that stand in need;
    suffer not that the beggar
putteth up his petition in vain.
    Perhaps thou shalt say:
The man has brought upon himself his misery.
    But I say unto you, whosoever doeth this,
the same hath great cause to repent.[4]

---

1. D&C 112:11
2. Jacob 2:17
3. Jacob 2:19
4. Mosiah 4:16-18

*I*mpart of your substance to the poor,
    every one according to that which you have,
such as feeding the hungry, clothing the naked,
    visiting the sick and administering to their relief,
both spiritually and temporally;
    and see that all these things
are done in wisdom and order.[1]

❦

*B*ehold, thou wilt remember the poor
    and consecrate of thy properties for their support.
And inasmuch as ye impart of your substance
    unto the poor, ye will do it unto me;
for inasmuch as ye do it unto the least of these,
    ye do it unto me.[2]

❦

*I*f there be properties in the hands of the church,
    or any individuals of it,
more than is necessary for their support,
    it shall be kept to administer
to those who have not,
    that everyone who has need
may be amply supplied.[3]

❦

*I*f anyone shall give unto you a coat, or a suit,
    take the old and give it unto the poor,
and go on your way rejoicing.[4]

❦

---

1. Mosiah 4:26-27   3. D&C 42:33
2. D&C 42:30-31, 38   4. D&C 84:105

*J*f any shall take of the abundance which I have made,
   and impart not, according to the law of my gospel,
unto the poor and needy,
   they shall, with the wicked,
lift up their eyes in hell,
   being in torment.[1]

⊰⊱

Calls to Reject Materialism

*A*nd it came to pass that I looked
   and beheld many nations and kingdoms;
I also saw gold and silver, and silks and scarlets,
   and fine-twined linen
and all manner of precious clothing.
   And the angel spake unto me, saying:
Behold the gold and the silver,
   and the silks and the scarlets,
and the fine-twined linen and the precious clothing,
   are the desires of they who belong not
to the covenant people of the Lord.[2]

⊰⊱

*W*o unto the rich;
   for because they are rich,
they despise the poor and persecute the meek,
   and their hearts are upon their treasures.
Wherefore, their treasure is their god.[3]

⊰⊱

---

1. D&C 104:18   2. 1 Ne. 13:1, 7-8; 14:10, 14   3. 2 Ne. 9:30

Do not spend money for that which is of no worth,
    nor your labor for that which cannot satisfy.[1]

❧

The hand of providence
    hath smiled upon you most pleasingly,
that you have obtained many riches;
    and because some of you
have obtained more abundantly,
    ye are lifted up in the pride of your hearts,
because of the costliness of your apparel,
    and ye suppose that ye are better than others.
And now, do ye suppose
    that God justifieth you in this thing?
Behold, I say unto you, Nay.[2]

❧

Lay not up for yourselves treasures upon earth,
    where moth and rust corrupt,
and thieves break through and steal;
    for where your treasure is,
there will your heart be also.[3]

❧

Why do ye adorn yourselves
    with that which hath no life,
and suffer the hungry and the needy
    and the naked and the sick and the afflicted
to pass by you and notice them not?[4]

❧

---

1. 2 Ne. 9:51   3. 3 Ne. 13:19, 21
2. Jacob 2:13-14   4. Morm. 8:39

*T*hou shalt not be proud in thy heart;
　　let thy garments be plain,
and their beauty the beauty of the work
　　of thine own hands.[1]

※

*T*hou shalt not be idle,
　　for whosoever is idle shall not eat the bread
nor wear the garments of the laborer.[2]

※

*W*o unto you rich,
　　that will not give your substance to the poor,
for your riches will canker your souls!
　　Wo unto you poor,
whose eyes are full of greediness,
　　and who will not labor with your own hands!
But blessed are the poor who are pure in heart;
　　the fatness of the earth shall be theirs.[3]

※

I, the Lord, am not well pleased
　　with the inhabitants of Zion,
for there are idlers among them;
　　and their children are also growing up
　　in wickedness,
for their eyes are full of greediness.
　　These things ought not to be,
and must be done away from among them.[4]

※

*G*o ye out from Babylon.[5]

※

---

1. D&C 42:40　　　3. D&C 56:16-18　　　5. D&C 133:5
2. D&C 42:42　　　4. D&C 68:31-32

Calls to Prevent the Earth's Destruction

The time cometh, saith the Lamb of God,
  that I will work a great and a marvelous work
among the inhabitants of the earth,
  a work which shall be everlasting,
either on the one hand or the other—
  either to the convincing of them unto peace,
or unto their being brought down into destruction,
  both temporally and spiritually.[1]

I, the Lord, knowing the calamities
  which should come upon the inhabitants
  of the earth,
called upon my servant Joseph Smith, Jun.,
  and gave him commandments,
and also gave commandments to others,
  that inasmuch as my servants sought wisdom,
  they might be instructed;
and inasmuch as they sinned,
  they might be chastened;
and inasmuch as they were humble,
  they might be made strong
and blessed from on high.[2]

Woe shall come upon the inhabitants of the earth
  if they will not hearken unto my words.
For a desolating scourge shall go forth among them,
  if they mend not their ways,
until the earth is empty and the inhabitants thereof
  are consumed away and utterly destroyed.[3]

---

1. 1 Ne. 14:7   2. D&C 1:17-18, 26-28   3. D&C 5:5, 19

Promises of a Better World

Promises of Unity Among the World's Peoples

The Holy One gathereth his children
    from the four quarters of the earth;
he numbereth his sheep, and they know him,
    and there shall be one fold and one shepherd.[1]

I command all people,
    both in the east and in the west,
and in the north and in the south,
    and in the islands of the sea,
that they shall write the words
    which I shall speak unto them;
and it shall come to pass
    that my word shall be gathered in one.[2]

---

1. 1 Ne. 22:25   2. 2 Ne. 29:11, 14

The Lord doeth that which is good
    among the inhabitants of the earth;
and he inviteth them all to come unto him
    and partake of his goodness—
black and white, bond and free, male and female—
    for all are alike unto God.[1]

❧

These are the fulness of times,
    in the which I will gather together in one
all things which are on earth.
    Wherefore, lift up your hearts and rejoice.[2]

❧

There shall be gathered unto Zion
    out of every nation under heaven;
they shall not be at war one with another.[3]

❧

Promises of Peace

All nations, kindreds, tongues, and people
    shall dwell safely in the Holy One.[4]

❧

The Lord shall judge among the nations,
    and shall rebuke many people.
They shall beat their swords into plowshares,
    and their spears into pruning hooks;
nation shall not lift up sword against nation,
    neither shall they learn war any more.[5]

❧

---

1. 2 Ne. 26:33   3. D&C 45:69   5. 2 Ne. 12:4
2. D&C 27:13-15   4. 1 Ne. 22:28

Of the increase of government and peace
  there shall be no end;
it shall be established with judgment and justice
  from henceforth, even forever.
The zeal of the Lord of Hosts will perform this.[1]

୬୭

The peace of God rest upon you,
  and upon your houses and lands,
and upon your flocks and herds,
  and all that you possess,
and also your families,
  from this time forth and forever.[2]

୬୭

Thou shalt be far from oppression—
  thou shalt not fear—
and from terror, for it shall not come near thee.
  In righteousness shalt thou be established,
and great shall be the peace of thy children.[3]

୬୭

Yours shall be called a land of peace,
  a city of refuge, a place of safety.[4]

୬୭

I will give unto you favor and grace
  in the eyes of your enemies,
that you may rest in peace and safety.[5]

୬୭

---

1. 2 Ne. 19:7   3. 3 Ne. 22:13-14   5. D&C 105:25
2. Alma 7:27   4. D&C 45:66

Promises of Aid for the Poor

The poor shall feed,
    and the needy shall lie down in safety.[1]

The meek shall increase,
    and their joy shall be in the Lord;
the poor shall rejoice in the Holy One of Israel.[2]

I have heard your prayers,
    and the poor have complained before me.
The rich I have made, and all flesh is mine,
    and I am no respecter of persons.
I have made the earth rich,
    and I hold forth to give you greater riches.[3]

For this cause I have sent you:
    that a feast of fat things
might be prepared for the poor;
    yea, a feast of fat things,
of wine on the lees well refined,
    that the earth may know
that the words of the prophets shall not fail;
    that the poor may come in
unto the marriage of the Lamb
    and partake of the supper of the Lord,
prepared for the great day to come.[4]

---

1. 2 Ne. 24:30   3. D&C 38:16-18
2. 2 Ne. 27:30   4. D&C 58:6, 8, 11

J, the Lord, stretched out the heavens
and built the earth,
and all things therein are mine.
And it is my purpose to provide for my people,
for all things are mine.
Behold, this is the way that I, the Lord,
have decreed to provide for my people:
that the poor shall be exalted,
in that the rich are made low,
for the earth is full,
and there is enough and to spare.[1]

Promises of Justice

*T*hus saith the Lord:
I will contend with them that oppress thee.[2]

*W*here is the fury of the oppressor?
I am the Lord thy God;
the Lord of Hosts is my name.
I have put my words in thy mouth,
and have covered thee in the shadow of mine hand,
that I may lay the foundations of the earth,
and say unto Zion: Behold, thou art my people.[3]

*T*hou hast multiplied the nation and increased the joy,
for thou hast broken the yoke, and the staff,
and the rod of the oppressor.[4]

---

1. D&C 104:14-17
2. 2 Ne. 6:17-18
3. 2 Ne. 8:13, 15-16
4. 2 Ne. 19:3-4

The zeal of the Lord of Hosts
    will establish justice forever.[1]

⅌

There shall come forth a rod out of the stem of Jesse,
    and a branch shall grow out of his roots.
With righteousness shall he judge the poor,
    and reprove with equity for the meek of the earth.[2]

⅌

Look unto God with firmness of mind,
    and pray unto him with exceeding faith,
and he will plead your cause,
    and send down justice
upon those who seek you harm.[3]

⅌

He doth cry by the voice of his angels:
    I will come down among my people,
with equity and justice in my hands.[4]

⅌

I have sworn, and the decree hath gone forth,
    that I would let fall the sword of my indignation
in behalf of my people,
    who have been afflicted and persecuted.
Even as I have said, it shall come to pass,
    and all they who have mourned
shall be comforted.[5]

⅌

---

1. 2 Ne. 19:7   3. Jacob 3:1   5. D&C 101:1, 10, 14
2. 2 Ne. 21:1, 4   4. Alma 10:21

*R*ejoice and be exceeding glad;
  for your God will mete out a just recompense
upon the heads of all your oppressors.[1]

❧

*N*aught but peace, justice, and truth
  is the habitation of thy throne.[2]

❧

Promises of Deliverance

*T*he Lord is able to deliver us,
  for behold, he is mightier than all the earth.[3]

❧

*T*he captives of the mighty shall be taken away,
  and the prey of the terrible shall be delivered;
for the Mighty God shall deliver his covenant people.[4]

❧

*L*ift up your heads and rejoice:
  the Lord will deliver you out of bondage.[5]

❧

*L*ift up your heads and be of good comfort,
  for I will covenant with my people
and deliver them out of bondage.
  And I will also ease the burdens
which are put upon your shoulders,
  that ye may know of a surety that I, the Lord,
do visit my people in their afflictions.[6]

❧

---

1. D&C 127:3
2. Moses 7:31
3. 1 Ne. 4:1, 3
4. 2 Ne. 6:17
5. Mosiah 7:19, 33
6. Mosiah 24:13-14

*Y*e must needs be led out of bondage by power,
    and with a stretched-out arm.
Therefore, let not your hearts be faint,
    for I say unto you:
Mine angels shall go up before you,
    and also my presence,
and in time ye shall possess that which is yours.[1]

*A*lthough the influence of thine enemies
    should cast thee into trouble,
and into bars and walls,
    thou shalt be had in honor.
But for a small moment and thy voice
    shall be more terrible
in the midst of thine enemies
    than the fierce lion, because of thy righteousness;
and thy God shall stand by thee forever and ever.
    Therefore, hold on thy way.[2]

Promises of Renewal for the Earth

I will preserve thee, to establish the earth,
    and to cause to inherit the desolate heritages.
Your pastures shall be in all high places;
    you shall not hunger nor thirst,
neither shall the heat nor the sun smite you,
    for he that hath mercy on you
shall lead you, even by springs of water.[3]

---

1. D&C 103:17, 19-20   2. D&C 122:4, 9   3. 1 Ne. 21:8-10

*L*ift up thine eyes round about and behold;
>for thy waste and thy desolate places,
and the land of thy destruction,
>shall again be inhabited.[1]

❧

*T*he Lord shall comfort Zion;
>he will comfort all her waste places.
He will make her wilderness like Eden,
>and her desert like the garden of the Lord.[2]

❧

*H*ave I not made the fowls of heaven,
>and also the fish of the sea,
and the beasts of the mountain?
>Have I not made the earth?
Do I not hold the destinies of all the armies
>of the nations of the earth?
Therefore, will I not make desert places
>to bud and to blossom,
and to bring forth in abundance?[3]

❧

*I*n the barren deserts
>there shall come forth pools of living water;
and the parched ground
>shall no longer be a thirsty land.[4]

❧

---

1. 1 Ne. 21:18-19   3. D&C 117:6-7
2. 2 Ne. 8:3   4. D&C 133:29

The Cause of Zion

Prayers for Peace, Justice, and the Needy

O Lord, do not suffer that this people
shall be destroyed by the sword.[1]

*W*e ask thee, Holy Father,
to remember those
who have been greatly oppressed and afflicted;
our hearts flow out with sorrow
because of their grievous burdens.
Therefore we plead before thee
for their full and complete deliverance
from under this yoke.
Break it off, O Lord, break it off by thy power.[2]

O Lord, we delight not
in the destruction of our fellow beings;
their souls are precious before thee.[3]

---

1. Hel. 11:4   2. D&C 109:32-33, 47-48   3. D&C 109:43

*H*ave mercy, O Lord,
    upon all the nations of the earth.
Remember all people—
    all the poor, the needy
and afflicted ones of the earth.[1]

O God, how long shall thy hand be stayed,
    and thine eye behold the wrongs of thy people,
and thine ear be penetrated with their cries?
    Yea, O Lord, how long
shall they suffer these wrongs and oppressions
    before thine heart shall be softened toward them,
and thy bowels be moved with compassion
    toward them?[2]

*R*emember thy suffering children, O our God,
    and thy servants will rejoice in thy name forever.[3]

Examples of Service

*M*y soul hungered,
    and I kneeled down before my Maker,
and I cried unto him in prayer and supplication.
    And it came to pass that I began to feel a desire
for the welfare of my brothers and sisters;
    wherefore, I did pour out my whole soul unto God
    for them.[4]

1. D&C 109:54-55   3. D&C 121:6
2. D&C 121:1-3   4. Enos 1:4, 9

*A*nd the people of the church were commanded
    that they should impart of their substance,
according to that which they had:
    if they had more abundantly,
they should impart more abundantly;
    and of they that had but little,
but little should be required;
    and to they that had not should be given.[1]

*A*nd thus, in their prosperous circumstances,
    they did not send away any
who were naked, or hungry, or athirst, or sick,
    or that had not been nourished.
And they did not set their hearts upon riches;
    therefore, they were liberal to all,
both old and young, both male and female,
    whether out of the church or in the church,
having no respect of persons
    as to those who stood in need.[2]

*N*ow when they saw great this work of destruction
    among their fellow beings,
they were moved with compassion,
    and went and inquired of the Lord
what they should do.[3]

---

1. Mosiah 18:27   2. Alma 1:30   3. Alma 27:4, 11

Examples of Zion

And it came to pass that there were no contentions
    and disputations among the people,
but every one did deal justly one with another.
    And they had all things common among them;
therefore there were not rich and poor, bond and free,
    but they were all made free,
and partakers of the heavenly gift.[1]

The Lord called his people ZION,
    because they were of one heart and one mind,
and there were no poor among them.
    And the Lord blessed the land,
and they were blessed upon the mountains
    and upon the high places,
and did flourish.[2]

Promises to Those
Who Labor for the Cause of Zion

Blessed are they who shall seek
    to bring forth my Zion,
for they shall have the power of the Holy Ghost;
    and if they endure to the end,
they shall be lifted up at the last day.[3]

---

1. 4 Ne. 1:2-3   2. Moses 7:17-18   3. 1 Ne. 13:37

*S*eek to bring forth and establish the cause of Zion,
    and you shall be the means of doing much good
in this generation.[1]

❧

*S*eek to bring forth and establish my Zion,
    and you shall have eternal life,
which gift is the greatest of all the gifts of God.[2]

❧

I have inspired you to move the cause of Zion
    in mighty power for good;
your diligence I know, and your prayers I have heard.
    Yea, your weeping for Zion I have seen,
and I will cause that you shall mourn for her
    no longer;
for your days of rejoicing are come
    unto the manifestations of my blessings
upon your works.[3]

❧

*K*eep the covenants by which ye are bound,
    and I will cause the heavens
to shake for your good,
    and Zion shall rejoice upon the hills and flourish.[4]

❧

*I*f ye are willing to observe your covenants by sacrifice,
    I, the Lord, will cause you
to bring forth as a very fruitful tree
    which is planted in a goodly land,
by a pure stream,
    that yieldeth much precious fruit.[5]

❧

---

1. D&C 6:6, 8   3. D&C 21:7-8   5. D&C 97:8-9
2. D&C 14:6-7   4. D&C 35:24

Surely Zion cannot fall,
    neither be moved out of her place,
for God is there, and the hand of the Lord is there,
    and he hath sworn by the power of his might
to be her salvation and her high tower.
    Therefore, saith the Lord, let Zion rejoice,
for this is Zion: THE PURE IN HEART.
    And blessed are all the pure in heart,
for they shall see God.[1]

Let your heart be comforted concerning Zion,
    for all flesh is in mine hands;
be still and know that I am God.[2]

---

1. D&C 97:19-21; 3 Ne. 12:8   2. D&C 101:16

About the Author

The son of convert parents, John Charles Duffy is the first member of his family born into the LDS Church. His father used to work on a crew that constructed chapels for the Church, so John has lived in various parts of the United States, including California, New York, New Jersey, Pennsylvania, and Idaho. When he was 10, his family moved to Utah, which has been his home ever since.

From 1991-93, John served a mission in the Dominican Republic. During his mission John developed a heightened appreciation for the power the scriptures have to provide consolation, strength, and vision in the midst of challenges.

Following his mission, John completed a Bachelor of Arts in English at Brigham Young University, then a Master of Arts in the same field at the University of Utah.

In 1997, John returned to the Dominican Republic, where he spent a summer as an education volunteer in a program serving a cluster of isolated villages. There his duties included teaching English, organizing a pre-school, and helping to set up a computer center. As the only Latter-day Saint in the area, John again relied on the scriptures for spiritual support. The idea for writing this book grew out of that experience.

Since returning to the United States, John has worked as a college composition instructor in Salt Lake City. He also teaches night classes to immigrants learning English as a second language. He would like to return again to the Dominican Republic. John's published work has appeared in literary journals, as well as in BYU's *The Restored Gospel and Applied Christianity.*